Book 1

ACTIVE

Skills for Communication

Chuck Sandy • Curtis Kelly

Series Consultant:
Neil J. Anderson

T0349589

HEINLE
CENGAGE Learning

Australia • Brazil • Japan • Korea • Mexico • Singapore • Spain • United Kingdom • United States

HEINLE
CENGAGE Learning™

**ACTIVE Skills for Communication,
Student Book 1**
Sandy / Kelly / Anderson

Publisher: Andrew Robinson

Editorial Manager: Sean Bermingham

Development Editor: Ian Purdon

Associate Development Editor:
Stephen Greenfield

Director of Global Marketing: Ian Martin

Content Project Manager: Tan Jin Hock

Senior Print Buyer: Mary Beth Hennebury

Illustrator: Raketshop Design Studio

Compositor: Chrome Media Pte Ltd / C. Hanzie

Cover Designer: Chrome Media Pte Ltd /
M. Chong

Cover Images: All photos from Shutterstock,
except bottom (Photos.com)

Photo Credits

Photos.com: pages 15, 17, 21 (top and bottom row), 23 (bottom row left), 24 (far left and far right), 26, 28 (1st column: all, 2nd column: 3rd and 5th from top), 31 (left and center left), 32, 33, 37, 39, 48, 49, 51, 54 (top row and 2nd row right), 58 (all except top row left and bottom row left), 60 (left), 67, 69 (top row left and center), 74, 75, 81 (top and bottom), 84, 100, 102 (all except 3rd from top), 109, 115; Index Open: pages 21 (center row), 23 (all except bottom row left), 24 (center left and center right), 28 (2nd column: 2nd and 4th from top), 41, 54 (2nd row left and bottom row), 59 (center left and center right), 60 (right), 83, 114; Chiu Hoi Kin: page 22, 28 (2nd column: top); Shutterstock: pages 30, 52, 77, 82; Ian Purdon: page 31 (center right); Photo Objects: pages 40, 50, 56, 57, 58 (top row left and bottom row left), 59 (far left and far right), 60 (center), 63 (center), 69 (all except top row left and center), 85, 90, 110; Dawn Elwell: page 63 (left); iStockphoto: pages 63 (right), 81 (center), 89, 91, 102 (3rd from top)

Student Book ISBN-13: 978-1-4130-2031-1
Student Book ISBN-10: 1-4130-2031-3
Book + Student Audio CD ISBN-13: 978-1-4240-0908-4
Book + Student Audio CD ISBN-10: 1-4240-0908-1

Heinle
25 Thomson Place
Boston, Massachusetts 02210
USA

Cengage Learning is a leading provider of customized learning solutions with office locations around the globe, including Singapore, the United Kingdom, Australia, Mexico, Brazil, and Japan. Locate our local office at:
international.cengage.com/region

Cengage Learning products are represented in Canada by Nelson Education, Ltd.

Visit Heinle online at **elt.heinle.com**
Visit our corporate website at **www.cengage.com**

Printed in Canada
1 2 3 4 5 6 7 8 9 10   12 11 10 09 08

DEDICATION AND ACKNOWLEDGMENTS

This book is dedicated to our families who have patiently endured our long periods of writing, and who have helped so much along the way with comments, suggestions, love, and support. We'd also like to dedicate this book to our students over the years for bearing with us as we tried out early versions of the activities that became ACTIVE Skills for Communication. By teaching us what learning is, they helped shape the ideas from which this course has arisen. Thanks go, too, to our editors at Cengage Learning, who have supported this project from the time it was first proposed several years ago. Their belief in our approach and vision for the course has been an enormous blessing. Particular thanks go to Chris Wenger, who first embraced the idea of ACTIVE Skills for Communication, Sean Bermingham and Guy De Villiers, who helped shape our approach, and Ian Purdon, who tirelessly worked with us through each and every page of the many versions of each unit. We could not have done it without you.

Our hope is that teachers around the world can use this series as a way to engage and motivate their learners, and that their students will be as successful in doing the activities and as enriched by them as our students have been.

We appreciate enormously the input we received from students and teachers in Korea, Thailand, Taiwan, Japan, Brazil, and the United States, including Oral Communication students at Osaka Gakuin and Heian Jogakuin Universities, and Oral Strategies students at Chubu University. We would especially like to thank Dr. Yoshiyasu Shirai, Anne Shirai, Daryl Aragaki, and Rex Tanimoto at Osaka Gakuin University.

Chuck Sandy & Curtis Kelly

Reviewers

Daryl Aragaki, Osaka Gakuin University; **Mayumi Asaba**, Osaka Gakuin University; **Rima Bahous**, Lebanese American University; **Phillip Barkman**, Asia University; **Edmar da Silva Falcão**, CEI—Centro De Ensino De Idioma; **Muriel Fujii**, Osaka Gakuin University; **John Gebhardt**, Ritsumeikan University; **Chris Hammond**, Kyoto Gakuen University; **Ann-Marie Hadzima**, National Taiwan University; **Brian Heldenbrand**, Jeonju University; **Caroline C. Hwang**, National Taipei University of Technology; **Mitsuyo Ito**, Osaka Gakuin University; **Hiroshi Izumi**, Tomigaoka Super English High School; **Kirsten Johannsen**, ELT specialist, the United States; **Leina Jucá**, MAI English; **Steve Jugovich**, Seikei Sports University; **Yuco Kikuchi**, English Pier School owner; **Michelle Misook Kim**, Kyung Hee University; **Kevin Knight**, Kanda University of International Studies; **Sumie Kudo**, Osaka Gakuin; **Hae Chin Moon**, Korea University; **Adam Murray**, Tokyo Denki University; **Heidi Nachi**, Ritsumeikan University; **Miho Omori**, Keirinkan; **Bill Pellowe**, Kinki University; **Nigel Randell**, Ryukoku University; **Alex Rath**, Shih Hsin University; **Gregg Schroeder**, ELT specialist, Hong Kong; **Pornpimol Senawong**, Silpakorn University; **Jeffrey Shaffer**, Shimane University; **Kyoko Shirakata**, ELT specialist; **Masahiro Shirai**, Doshisha Girls' Junior and Senior High Schools; **Thang Siew Ming**, Universiti Kebangsaan Malaysia; **Stephen Slater**, ELT specialist; **Wang Songmei**, Beijing Institute of Education; **Scott Smith**, Kansai Gaidai University; **Joe Spear**, Hanbat National University; **Rex Tanimoto**, Osaka Gakuin University; **Ellen Tanoura**, Osaka Gakuin University; **Dave Tonetti**, Kyung Hee University; **Matthew Walsh**, Momoyama Gakuin High School and Ikeda High School; **James Webb**, Kansai Gaidai University; **Nancy Yu**, ELT specialist

SCOPE AND SEQUENCE

Unit	Challenge	Skills	Fluency	Language
1. Class Album *Page 13*	Interviewing a classmate and making a class album	Greeting people; Sharing personal information	Asking politely with *May I ask . . .*	**Personal information** name, email address, hobbies & interests, etc. **Wh- questions & answers** What's your last name? It's Garcia. **Yes/No questions & answers** Do you have a pet? Yes, I do. I have a dog. **Clarifying phrases** How do you spell that?; Can you say that again, please?
2. Favorite Photos *Page 21*	Sharing personal photos and information	Describing people, places, and events	Asking follow-up questions	**Present simple tense questions & answers** Who's this? That's my friend, Andrew. **Past simple tense questions & answers** Where were you? We were at a baseball game. **People, places, & events** friend, office, baseball game, etc. **Adjectives** kind, interesting, exciting, etc.
3. Personal Goals *Page 29*	Making an action plan and presenting a personal goal	Explaining intentions and future plans	Giving advice with *should*	**Intentions with** *would like to/really want to* **+ infinitive** I'd like to go to Thailand, because I want to learn how to cook Thai food. **Future with** *be going to* **+ infinitive** I'm going to find a cooking school. **Infinitives** live abroad, be fluent in English, work for a big company **Time expressions** someday, by November, this winter, etc.
Project 1. Self-Improvement Plan *Page 37*		**Recycling themes and language from Unit 3** Making and explaining a self-improvement plan poster		
4. Believe It or Not *Page 39*	Telling short stories in a true/lie game	Describing past experiences	Showing interest	**Past simple tense** I went to a concert with my sister. **Present perfect tense with** *Have you ever . . .* Have you ever gone camping? No, I haven't. **Time expressions** last year, one day, two years ago, etc. **Adjectives** awful, amazing, great, etc.
5. Where I Grew Up *Page 47*	Making a map and taking classmates on a tour	Describing past routines and important memories	Describing in detail	**Past routines with** *used to* **+** *when* I used to go to the park when I was little. **Past simple tense** What did you do there? **Present simple tense** Do you still go there? **Locations** park, store, high school, etc.
6. Bargain Shopper *Page 55*	Bargaining for goods in a shopping simulation	Describing goods; Buying and selling goods	Refusing an offer	**Bargaining expressions** May I help you?, How much is it?, That's too much., etc. **Shopping goods** watch, briefcase, necklace, etc. **Adjectives** popular, gold, beautiful, etc. **Locations** night market, flea market, online auction site, etc.
Project 2. Flea Market *Page 63*		**Recycling themes and language from Unit 6** Selling, buying, and bargaining		

Unit	Challenge	Skills	Fluency	Language
7. The Perfect Gift *Page 65*	Explaining an imaginative gift idea	Describing significant people and showing gratitude	Giving and receiving	***Would like to* + infinitive to express wishes** I'd like to give Emma a one-year study trip . . . ***Because* and *for* + *ing* to give reasons** I'd like to give Ana a gift because she's a good friend. I'd like to thank you for reminding me about . . . **Special occasions** wedding, Mother's Day, Valentine's Day **Expressing thanks** You're so kind., That's very thoughtful of you., etc.
8. Party Planner *Page 73*	Planning a party with a partner and inviting classmates	Giving invitations and asking for information	Accepting and declining invitations	**Future with *be going to* + infinitive** We're going to cook some burgers and hot dogs. **Asking for a suggestion with *should*** Should I bring my camera? **Inviting, accepting, and declining expressions** Do you want to come? Yes, I'd love to. / I'm sorry. I can't., etc. **Parties and gatherings** New Year's party, birthday party, barbecue, etc.
9. Music Profile *Page 81*	Interviewing a classmate and presenting a music profile	Sharing information on music tastes	Reporting with *He said . . .* and *He told her . . .*	**Wh- questions & answers** What kind of music are you into? I love hip-hop. **Yes/No questions & answers** Do you ever listen to classical music? Sometimes. **Recommendations** What's good to listen to when you feel down? I recommend Beyoncé. **Music genres** soul music, classical music, rock music, etc.
Project 3. Radio DJ *Page 89*		**Recycling themes and language from Unit 9** Making a DJ recording and presenting a favorite song		
10. Style Makeover *Page 91*	Interviewing a classmate and presenting a new clothing style	Describing clothing and styles	Giving advice politely with *Why don't you try . . .*	**Present simple tense** I like to wear casual clothes. **Present progressive tense** She's wearing a blue and white checked dress. **Adjectives and comparatives** styles, colors, more fashionable, etc. **Clothing items** pants, shirt, dress, etc.
11. Honesty *Page 99*	Telling and discussing dilemma situations	Describing difficult situations and giving opinions	Asking for clarification	**Present simple tense** Your best friend gets a new hairstyle. **Hypothetical questions & answers using *would*** What would you do? I would tell the truth. **Hypothetical questions with *Would you* (ever) . . .** Would you ever skip school to do something fun? Sure, why not?
12. Making Things Better *Page 107*	Discussing a problem at school and presenting the solution	Describing problems, asking for advice, and making suggestions	Encouraging others to speak	**Result clauses with *so*** We don't have enough homework, so I'm not learning much. **Determiners *not enough, too much, too many, more*** We don't have enough homework., We have too much homework., We have too many social events., We need more choices. **Suggestions with *should* and *could*** What should I do? You could drink some coffee.
Project 4. What I Have Learned *Page 115*		**Evaluating progress and successes from Unit 10** Self-evaluation		
Audio Scripts and "Spoken English"	*Page 117*			

WELCOME!

To learners:

Welcome to *Active Skills for Communication*. Here are some suggestions to help you get as much as possible from this course.

- ▶ First, be active. Make using and learning English your personal goal. Be active in learning English by being active in using it.
- ▶ Second, don't be afraid to make mistakes. Each mistake is a step toward learning.
- ▶ Third, be aware of how communication involves critical thinking and decision making. This thinking is an important part of learning.
- ▶ Fourth, develop learning strategies. Decide what you need to learn. Then, find the ways to learn that best fit your style.
- ▶ Fifth, learn how the different parts of a unit work, so that you can get the most out of them.
- ▶ In short, be positive toward communicating in English. There are many new experiences waiting for you in the pages that follow.

Chuck Sandy & Curtis Kelly

To teachers:

What are the basic characteristics of this course?

First, it is goal-oriented. Each unit builds toward a final speaking activity, such as an interview, a presentation, a game, a role-play, or a discussion. These *Challenge* activities are more than straightforward language exercises—they foster meaningful interaction between students and are based on real situations language learners face both inside and outside of the classroom.

Second, it is strategy-oriented. Interacting in English requires a greater repertoire of skills than just being able to produce the right grammar and vocabulary. It requires learners to identify goals, choose strategies, speak expressively, and respond appropriately. Learners are encouraged to think critically about the language they are learning, thereby helping them integrate communication strategies into real interactions.

Finally, it makes learners active. Personalized speaking activities throughout the course give learners ownership of their interactions and their learning. When students use English to relate real experiences, frame real opinions, and respond genuinely to others, English becomes more than something to study. It becomes something to broaden their perspectives.

ARE YOU AN *ACTIVE* COMMUNICATOR?

Before you use this book to develop your communication skills, think about your speaking and listening habits, and your strengths and weaknesses when communicating in English. Check [✔] the statements that are true for you.

1. I look for chances to use English.
   ☐ Start of course   ☐ End of course

2. I sometimes speak English with people who speak my first language.
   ☐ Start of course   ☐ End of course

3. I enjoy communicating in English with English speakers.
   ☐ Start of course   ☐ End of course

4. I think communicating in English is fun.
   ☐ Start of course   ☐ End of course

5. I tell myself "speaking English is easy."
   ☐ Start of course   ☐ End of course

6. I don't mind making pronunciation, vocabulary, or grammar mistakes.
   ☐ Start of course   ☐ End of course

7. If the listener does not understand something, I try to say it in a different way.
   ☐ Start of course   ☐ End of course

8. I listen to how other people say things in English, such as in movies or music.
   ☐ Start of course   ☐ End of course

9. When I listen, I try to get the message rather than try to understand every word.
   ☐ Start of course   ☐ End of course

10. If I can't understand what someone is saying very well, I guess.
    ☐ Start of course   ☐ End of course

11. I'm a good listener—I listen carefully to what other people are saying.
    ☐ Start of course   ☐ End of course

12. I don't answer questions with just one word, such as "yes" or "no." I say more.
    ☐ Start of course   ☐ End of course

13. I try to think in English before speaking, rather than translate from my language.
    ☐ Start of course   ☐ End of course

14. I participate in class, talking as much as I can.
    ☐ Start of course   ☐ End of course

15. I sometimes review what we study in class at home.
    ☐ Start of course   ☐ End of course

16. I plan to travel to an English-speaking country if I can.
    ☐ Start of course   ☐ End of course

At the end of the course, answer the quiz again to see if you have become a more fluent, active communicator.

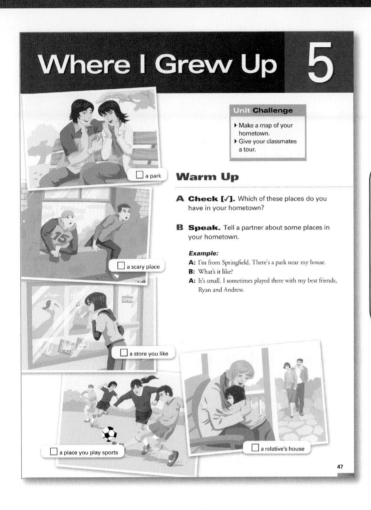

1. Each unit begins with the *Warm Up*. This page gets you thinking about the unit topic, and will help you talk about your life and your experiences. For example, there are units on your personal goals, your hometown, and your tastes in music.

2. The *Challenge Preview* demonstrates what you are going to do in the *Challenge*—that's the major speaking activity at the end of the unit. This page presents the language you will need to do the *Challenge*. Listen to some students doing the *Challenge*, and do the activities to help you prepare.

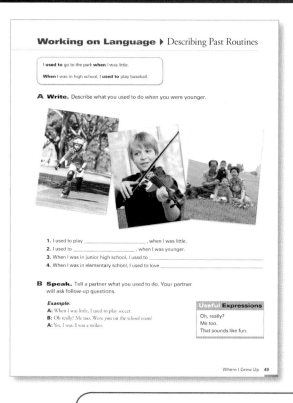

Working on Language ▸ Describing Past Routines

> I **used to** go to the park **when** I was little.
>
> **When** I was in high school, I **used to** play baseball.

A Write. Describe what you used to do when you were younger.

1. I used to play _____ , when I was little.
2. I used to _____ , when I was younger.
3. When I was in junior high school, I used to _____
4. When I was in elementary school, I used to love _____

B Speak. Tell a partner what you used to do. Your partner will ask follow-up questions.

Example:
A: When I was little, I used to play soccer.
B: Oh really? Me too. Were you on the school team?
A: Yes, I was. I was a striker.

Useful Expressions
Oh, really?
Me too.
That sounds like fun.

3. *Working on Language* teaches you what to say in the *Challenge*. Simple charts and activities help you structure your ideas, and allow you to talk about yourself with your classmates. *Useful Expressions* also help you interact with your classmates more freely.

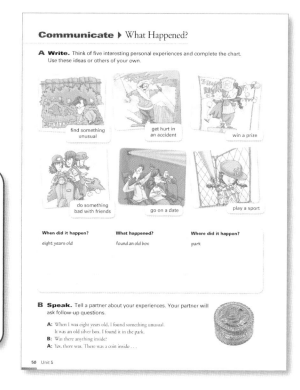

Communicate ▸ What Happened?

A Write. Think of five interesting personal experiences and complete the chart. Use these ideas or others of your own.

find something unusual | get hurt in an accident | win a prize
do something bad with friends | go on a date | play a sport

When did it happen?	What happened?	Where did it happen?
eight years old	found an old box	park

B Speak. Tell a partner about your experiences. Your partner will ask follow-up questions.

A: When I was eight years old, I found something unusual. It was an old silver box. I found it in the park.
B: Was there anything inside?
A: Yes, there was. There was a coin inside . . .

4. *Communicate* extends what you have learned in the unit so far. It also gives you more opportunities to talk with your classmates about the unit topic.

Note to teacher: The end of this page is a great place to stop if you are teaching the unit in two lessons.

Working on Fluency ▸ Describing in Detail

A [10] Listen. You are going to do a relaxation exercise. It will help you remember a place, or maybe a person, or an event. Close your eyes and listen.

B Write. Make notes on what you remembered: a person, a place, an event, a sound, a smell, etc.

C Speak. Get into groups and talk about your experiences. Your classmates will ask these and other follow-up questions. Take turns.

How did you feel? What was it like?
What special place did you remember? Why?
What did you see? Did you smell or hear anything?

Level Up!
See page 54.

5. *Working on Fluency* helps you speak more fluently and do the *Challenge* more successfully. For example, in one unit, you'll learn how to ask follow-up questions to extend your conversations in English.

Listen to the conversations on the CD and then engage in deeper conversations with your classmates.

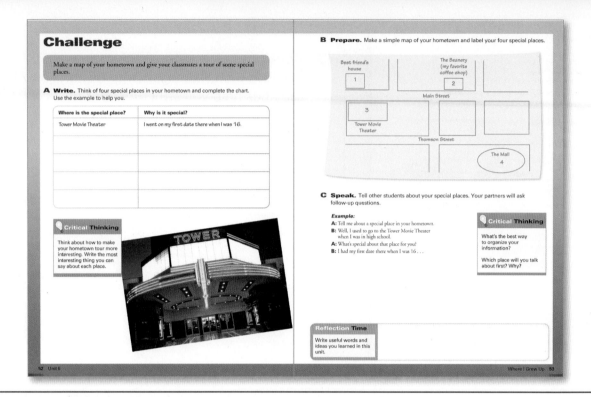

6. The *Challenge* is the major speaking activity at the end of the unit. Each *Challenge* is based on a situation you're likely to face, or a skill you're likely to need, to communicate in English—both inside and outside of the classroom. The *Challenges* include games, interviews, and role-plays.

Some *Challenges* will ask you to make a presentation. Read the presentation tips and practice them to become a confident and effective presenter.

When doing the *Challenge*, don't worry about using perfect English. Instead, concentrate on getting the *Challenge* done using only English. The *Challenge* gets you to use everything you learned to really *communicate* with your classmates.

The reflection time helps you organize and record language that's important to you.

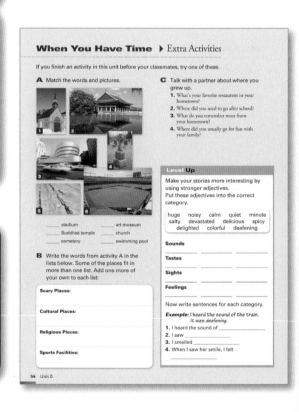

7. Try the fun *When You Have Time* activities when you finish an activity before your classmates. Some can be done alone, and others are speaking activities to be done in pairs.

The *Level Up* material gets you to think about what you have learned, and develop your language skills.

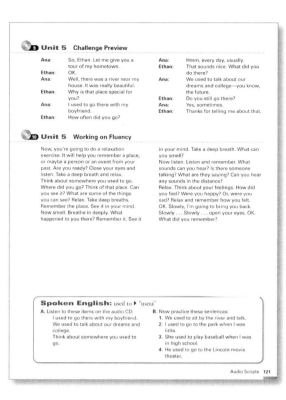

Communicate More

At the back of the book, the *Spoken English* material (pages 117–128) gets you thinking about how native speakers of American English really talk. When speaking, native speakers of American English often change the way they pronounce certain words and phrases.

Projects

The *Projects* take learning beyond the classroom. You'll do research and prepare outside of class, and then present your project to your classmates. Each project will give you the chance to express yourself. There are four in this student book: a flea market, a radio show, a self-improvement plan, and a self-evaluation.

CLASSROOM LANGUAGE

Language you will hear in the class:

Open your books to Unit 1.

Listen to the conversation.

Compare answers with a partner.

Find a partner.

Let's do part A.

Look at the *Warm-up* page.

Make groups of four.

Work by yourself.

Language you will want to use in class:

Luis

Could you say that again, please?

Did you say (page 12)?

What does _____ mean?

How do you say _____ in English?

Kirsten

Could you explain this activity again?

How do you spell that?

Steven

Sang-mi

We've finished the activity.

What should we do next?

Language you will use to work with a partner or in groups:

Yumi

I'll go first.

It's your turn.

That's a good idea!

Ana

What do you think?

How about you?

Thanks for telling me.

Ethan

Class Album

Unit Challenge

▸ Interview a classmate.
▸ Make a class album.

Warm Up

Speak. Introduce yourself to as many classmates as you can in five minutes. Then tell the class all the names you remember.

Challenge Preview

A  **Listen.**
Some students are doing the Challenge at the end of this unit. Kirsten is asking Luis some questions. How well do they know each other? Check [✓] the correct answer.

☐ They are old friends.
☐ They are new classmates.
☐ They are brother and sister.

> May I ask you some questions?

> Sure, Kirsten.

B **Write and listen again.** Fill in the missing pronouns "you" or "your" to complete the questions. Then listen to check your ideas.

Kirsten:	What's _____ last name, **Luis**?
Luis:	It's **Garcia**.
Kirsten:	How do _____ spell that?
Luis:	**G-A-R-C-I-A.**
Kirsten:	Did _____ say **G-A-R-C-I-A**?
Luis:	Yes, that's right.
Kirsten:	OK. What's _____ cell phone number?
Luis:	It's **090-555-1212**.
Kirsten:	Can _____ say that again, please?
Luis:	Sure. **090-555-1212**.

C **Speak.** Practice the conversation with a partner. Then change the words in **red** to talk about yourself.

Working on Language ▶ Asking Questions

A Write. Complete the questions and answers, using the words below.

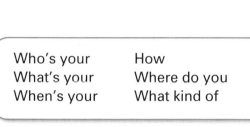

Who's your	How
What's your	Where do you
When's your	What kind of

GK10@fast.com	hip-hop music
Kim Yoon-jin	21
June 19	near school

1. _____What's your_____ email address? It's _____
2. _____ old are you? I'm _____
3. _____ birthday? It's _____
4. _____ music are you interested in? I'm into _____
5. _____ live? I live _____
6. _____ favorite movie star? Maybe _____

B Match. Draw lines from each question to a "yes" and "no" answer.

1. Do you have a pet?

2. Can you play tennis?

3. Are you from China?

No, I can't, but I can play badminton.

Yes, I do. I have a dog.

Yes, I can, but not very well.

No, I don't, but I'd like one.

Yes, I am. I'm from Beijing.

No, I'm not. I'm from Seoul.

C Speak. Ask a partner questions from activities A and B. Your partner will answer with real information.

Example:
A: Where do you live?
B: I live downtown.
A: Oh really?

B: Do you have a pet?
A: Yes, I do. I have a cat.
B: Me too.

Useful Expressions

Oh really?
That's interesting.
Me too.
Me neither.

Communicate ▶ Are We the Same?

A Write. What questions can you ask a new classmate? Use these or your own ideas. Then share your ideas with the class.

travels?

family?

favorites?

likes and dislikes?

Example: How many brothers and sisters do you have?

1. _____

2. _____

3. _____

4. _____

5. _____

B Speak. Get into groups. Ask your classmates questions. Find things you have in common and write them down.

Example:

A: How many brothers and sisters do you have, Steven?

B: I have one sister.

A: Oh really? So do I.

Name	We both . . .
Steven	have a sister.

Working on Fluency ▶ Asking Polite Questions

> Notice how the word order changes in Wh- questions (what, when, who, which, where, why how).
>
> Where are you from?
> ▼
> **May I ask** where you are from?
>
> *Sure. I'm from New York.*
> *Sorry. I'd rather not say.*

A **Listen.** These new classmates are getting to know each other. Check [✓] the questions that you hear. Then write the answers.

1 Julie
- ☐ What's your phone number?
- ☐ May I ask what your cell phone number is?

Answer
_____

2 Andrew
- ☐ How tall are you?
- ☐ May I ask how tall you are?

Answer
_____

3 Emma
- ☐ How old are you?
- ☐ May I ask how old you are?

Answer
_____

B Check [✓]. Which questions do you think are OK to ask students in your class? Compare your answers with a partner.

- ☐ Hobbies
- ☐ Nationality
- ☐ Weight
- ☐ Job
- ☐ Phone number
- ☐ Age
- ☐ Home address
- ☐ Height
- ☐ Favorites
- ☐ Family

C Write and speak. Write three Wh- questions using "May I ask." Then practice your questions with some classmates.

Level Up!
See page 20.

Example: May I ask where you are from?

1. _____
2. _____
3. _____
4. _____

Challenge

Interview a partner, complete the worksheet, and make a class album.

**Critical Thinking**

Look at the question prompts on the worksheet. When should you use "May I ask . . . ?"

A Write. Look at the worksheet on the next page. Then prepare questions for items 2 to 6. Use the example below to help you.

1. _What's your name?_____
2. _____
3. _____
4. _____
5. _____
6. _____

B Write. Look at the worksheet again. Then prepare questions for items 7 to 15, using your own ideas.

7. _____
8. _____
9. _____
10. _____
11. _____
12. _____
13. _____
14. _____
15. _____

C Speak. Interview a partner and complete your worksheet.

Example:

A: What's your name?
B: Jill Barr.
A: How do you spell "Barr?"
B: B-A-R-R.

Reflection Time

Write useful words and ideas you learned in this unit.

CLASS ALBUM

1. **NAME:**

2. **NICKNAME:**

3. **PHONE:**

4. **EMAIL:**

5. **HOME:**

6. **BIRTHDAY:**

**PICTURE OF YOUR PARTNER
(DRAW IT)**

7. **FAVORITE:** _____

8. **FAVORITE:** _____

9. **FAVORITE:** _____

10. **INTERESTS & HOBBIES:**

11. **SPECIAL TALENTS:**

12. **FUTURE:**

13-15. **OTHER INTERESTING POINTS:**

Optional Activity: Photocopy the completed worksheets and make a class album. Make copies for everyone in the class.

When You Have Time ▶ Extra Activities

If you finish an activity in this unit before your classmates, try one of these.

A Guess the question words: where, what, how, which, why.

How _____ _____

_____ _____

B Do the quiz. How well do you know your brother, sister, or best friend? Complete the chart.

☐ Brother ☐ Sister ☐ Best friend	
Name	
Nickname	
Age	
Birthday	
Pet	
Cell/Home phone	
Email address	
Favorite color	
Favorite dish (food)	
Junior high school	

C Talk with a partner about your family.

1. How many people are in your family?
2. How many sisters and brothers do you have?
3. Where do they live?
4. Who are you closest to in your family?

Level Up

You can also ask other types of questions using "May I ask."

Example:
Are you single? ▶
May I ask if you are single?

Do you have any children? ▶
May I ask if you have any children?

Make these questions more polite. Then practice your questions with a partner.

1. Are you married?
   _____
2. Do you have a boyfriend/girlfriend?
   _____
3. Do you live alone?
   _____
4. Do you like studying English?
   _____
5. Are you interested in politics?
   _____

Favorite Photos 2

a

Unit Challenge

▶ Show your classmates some personal photos.

Warm Up

Number. Match the photos with these sentences.

1. We finally won!
2. She was always so kind.
3. She can't talk, but I usually understand her.
4. We always did crazy things together.
5. That was a great trip!

b

c

d

e

Challenge Preview

A 🔊 **3 Listen.** In the Challenge, Ethan and Yumi are showing each other their photos. What does Ethan's photo show?

- ☐ a bad day
- ☐ a good memory
- ☐ some important information

This is a picture of me when I was in high school.

B 🔊 **3 Write and listen again.** Fill in the missing words that start these questions. Then listen to check your ideas.

> was   do   where   who

Yumi: OK. _____ 's this?

Ethan: That's my friend, **Andrew**.

Yumi: _____ were you?

Ethan: We were **at a baseball game**.

Yumi: _____ it fun?

Ethan: Yeah, it was a great day.

Yumi: _____ you still see **Andrew**?

Ethan: Sometimes. He's **a cool guy**.

C Speak. Practice the conversation with a partner. Then change the words in **red** to talk about this photo.

▶ Mark
▶ an amusement park
▶ a good friend

Working on Language ▶ Describing Photos

	What or Who	**More Information**
This is a picture of	my sister and I. my apartment.	We were on vacation in China. It's really small.

A Write. Describe each picture with two sentences. Use the ideas below to get started.

my parents' house	my high school graduation	my mom and dad
They love camping.	It's really large.	I was so proud.

1. This is a picture of _____

2. _____

3. _____

4. _____

5. _____

B Speak. Pretend the photos are your photos. Tell a partner about them.

Example:

A: This is a picture of my mom and dad. They love camping.

B: That's interesting.

Level Up! See page 28.

> **Useful Expressions**
>
> That's really interesting.
> That's really nice.
> That sounds exciting.

Communicate ▶ Who's This?

A Number and speak. Look at the photos, read the sentences, and number the follow-up questions. Then practice the conversations with a partner. Try to answer the follow-up questions.

That's Ms. Jones. She was my high school teacher.

That's Carl. He was my boyfriend.

That's Abby. She's my little sister.

That's Mark. He's my roommate.

_____ She's cute. Are you close?

_____ Nice photo. What did she teach?

_____ He was? Do you still see him sometimes?

_____ Cool guy! Do you study together?

B Speak. Tell a partner about three people you know. Write their names (or draw a picture of each person). Your partner will ask questions.

Name: _____   Name: _____   Name: _____

Example:

A: That's my brother, Chan.

B: Is he your younger brother?

A: No. He's older than me.

B: What does he do?

A: He works in an office.

Working on Fluency ▶ Asking Follow-up Questions

A 🔘 **4** **Listen.** Kirsten is talking about one of her favorite photos. Check [✓] the six follow-up questions you hear.

- ☐ How old is she?
- ☐ What's she holding?
- ☐ Where did you take it?
- ☐ Is that her favorite sport?
- ☐ Is that a volleyball?
- ☐ Did she have a game that day?
- ☐ When did you take this?
- ☐ Do you have any other sisters?

B **Write.** Look at Kirsten's other favorite photos. Think of three follow-up questions for each photo.

This is a picture of my sister's wedding.

This is a picture of my friend's beach barbecue.

1. _____
2. _____
3. _____

1. _____
2. _____
3. _____

C **Speak.** Find a partner. Pretend one of the photos in activity B is yours. Your partner will ask questions about it.

Challenge

Show your classmates some of your favorite photos and talk about them.

A Write. Choose one of your photos and think of four questions a classmate could ask about it. Then think of the answers.

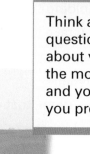

Think about what questions people will ask about your photos. Write the most likely questions, and your answers, to help you prepare.

Example:

Question: Where were you?

Answer: I was in the park with my grandparents.

1. Question: _____

Answer: _____

2. Question: _____

Answer: _____

3. Question: _____

Answer: _____

4. Question: _____

Answer: _____

Reflection Time

Write useful words and ideas you learned in this unit.

B **Show your photos.** Follow these instructions.

1. Make two circles, like the picture.

2. In pairs, a student in the outside circle shows a photo to a student in the inside circle.

3. The pairs discuss the photo.

4. Then the other student shows a photo.

5. The teacher says "Change!" Students in the outside circle move to their right.

6. Continue the activity, discussing other photos with new partners.

When You Have Time ▶ Extra Activities

If you finish an activity in this unit before your classmates, try one of these.

A Do the word search. Find these words:

camera   video
snapshot   slide
~~frame~~   photo

T	O	T	V	T	L	K	C
O	T	O	E	D	W	Z	A
E	O	H	E	C	I	M	M
M	H	S	N	D	C	C	E
A	P	P	S	R	I	M	R
R	J	A	P	L	U	V	A
F	R	N	C	B	I	R	L
Y	C	S	L	T	N	D	F
W	U	A	W	E	A	D	E

B Do the quiz. Guess the objects.

___notebook___   _____   _____

_____   _____

C Talk with a partner about your photos.

1. Where do you keep your old photos?
2. Do you have any photos in your wallet or purse?
3. Do you have any photos on your walls or desk?
4. Do you have any photo albums?

Level Up

You can talk about actions when you describe a photo.

Example:
I **was** visit**ing** Disneyland with my friend.

Answer these questions. Then practice with a partner.

1. What are they doing?
   They _____ _____ in Yellowstone National Park.

2. What were you doing?
   We _____ _____

3. What was she doing?
   _____ _____ _____

4. What was she doing?
   _____ _____ _____

Personal Goals

☐ live abroad

Warm Up

A Rank. What are your future goals? Rank the pictures ✓ = want to do, ✓✓ = really want to do, ✗ = don't want to do.

B Speak. Ask some classmates about their future goals.

Example:
A: Do you want to live abroad someday?
B: Yes, I do. How about you?
A: Me too.

☐ be famous

☐ work for a big company

☐ be fluent in English

MOVERS

☐ move to a different city

Challenge Preview

A  **5 Listen.** In the Challenge, Sang-mi is explaining a personal goal. What would Sang-mi like to do?

☐ learn how to cook Thai food

☐ open a Thai restaurant

☐ save $3,000

B **5 Write and listen again.** Fill in the missing time expressions. Then listen to check your ideas.

> tonight   by November   this winter

Sang-mi: I'd like to **go to Thailand** _____.

Steven: Really? Why?

Sang-mi: Because I want to **learn how to cook Thai food.**

Steven: So, what's your plan?

Sang-mi: Well, _____, I'm going to **find a cooking school** on the Internet.

Steven: That's a good idea.

Sang-mi: Then, _____, I'm going to **book an air ticket and a hotel room.**

C **Speak.** Practice the conversation with a partner. Then change the words in **red** to talk about this photo.

My Plan
▶ buy a scooter
▶ ride it to school.
▶ look for a part-time job
▶ save $1,000

Working on Language ▶ Describing Future Goals

What	When
I **would like to** go to Thailand	next month.
I **really want to** get married	this year.
	within five years.
	before I graduate.
	someday.

A Write. Think of five personal goals, using these ideas or others of your own.

travel abroad?

have a child?

find a new job?

take the TOEIC® test?

Example: I would like to take the TOEIC test this year.

1. _____
2. _____
3. _____
4. _____
5. _____

B Speak. Tell a partner about the things you would like to do. Take turns.

Example:
A: I'd like to take the TOEIC test this year.
B: Great! Good luck!

Useful Expressions

Great! Good luck!
That sounds fun.
I had no idea!

Communicate ▶ Why?

A Speak and write. Get into groups and discuss these sentences. Think of as many reasons for each idea as you can. Then choose the best reason. Use the example below to help you.

1 We'd like to finish class early today, because . . .

we want to go to a movie together.

_____
_____
_____
_____
_____

2 We'd like to make a class blog or website, because . . .

_____
_____
_____
_____
_____
_____

B Write and speak. Look at your goals on page 31 and think of at least one reason for each goal. Then tell a partner about your plans.

Example: I'd like to take the TOEIC test this year, because I want to work abroad.

1. _____
2. _____
3. _____
4. _____
5. _____

Working on Fluency ▶ Asking for Advice

A 🔘 **6** **Listen.** Luis would like to visit Australia. What advice do his friends give him? Check [✓] the correct answers.

Luis should:

☐ go to a language school in Sydney.   ☐ talk to a travel agency.

☐ take the TOEFL® test.   ☐ buy travel insurance.

☐ save some cash.   ☐ get a cheap air ticket.

B **Write.** Give Luis two more suggestions.

Example: I think you should look for discount tickets on the Internet too.

1. _____

2. _____

C **Speak and write.** Get into groups. Have one student tell a goal from the previous page (or one of the goals below). Make as many suggestions as you can. Take notes.

Example:

A: I'd like to go to Egypt and visit the pyramids, so what should I do?

B: I think you should get a visa as soon as possible.

A: That's a good idea. Thanks. What else?

C: You should read some books about Egypt.

A: That sounds good too. Thank you.

go to Egypt

run a marathon

lose two kilos

become a singer

start a business

Challenge

Discuss one of your goals with a partner. Then make an action plan and present it to the class.

A **Write.** Think of one personal goal and complete the chart. Use the example below to help you.

What	When	Why
start a rock band	this year	to play at the school festival

B **Speak.** Tell a partner about your goal. Take turns thinking of things you should do. Write at least six ideas.

Example:

A: I'd like to start a rock band. So what should I do?

B: Well, first, you should find some musicians.

A: Yes, I'm going to put an ad in the newspaper for a singer and a drummer.

B: You should put some posters around campus, too.

A: Good idea. Thanks.

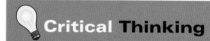 **Critical** **Thinking**

Think about the suggestions after you complete activity B. Are they helpful? Check the most useful ideas and number them in the best order.

Level Up!
See page 36.

C Prepare. Follow these instructions.

1. Make a poster.

start a

2. Write your goal.

4. Write when you are going to finish each task.

3. Write at least four things you are going to do.

Check when done:
- ☐ Put an ad in a newspaper for a singer and drummer
- ☐ Interview the singer and drummer
- ☐ Choose a name for the band
- ☐ Write three original songs and practice
- ☐ Give a free concert at school

By:
next March
next April
next April
May-August
September

D Present. Tell your classmates about your action plan. Your classmates will ask follow-up questions.

Presentation Tip

Make sure you introduce yourself to the audience at the start of your presentation.

Reflection Time

Write useful words and ideas you learned in this unit.

When You Have Time ▶ Extra Activities

If you finish an activity in this unit before your classmates, try one of these.

A Do the crossword puzzle.

Across

1. You should get a _____ if you want to go abroad.

3. You should have _____ if you want to make a big family.

4. You should practice _____ if you want to get a car license.

7. You should learn _____ if you want to live in France.

Down

2. You should _____ hard if you want to go to graduate school.

3. You shouldn't eat _____ if you want to lose weight.

5. You should be _____ to people if you want to make friends.

6. You should save _____ if you want to buy a car.

B Do the quiz. Think of one friend or classmate for each of these goals. Complete the sentences. Then check your answers.

_____ wants to be a company president.

_____ wants to be a TV star.

_____ wants to be rich and never work.

_____ wants to be a popular author.

_____ wants to be a child again.

C Talk with a partner about your dreams.

1. What do you want to become in the future?

2. What did you want to become when you were little?

3. Would you rather be rich or famous?

4. Are you happy now?

Level Up

You can talk about what you must do and what is important when you explain your goal:

Example:

I would like to go to Thailand to learn how to cook Thai food. ▶
I need to find a cooking school.
I have to book tickets.

Here are two goals. Put these goals into two lists. Then tell a partner about one of your goals — what you "have to" do and "need to" do.

Goal 1. I would like to go camping in Spain this summer.

Goal 2. I would like to learn ballroom dancing.

___1___ I have to save some money.

_____ I need to choose a class.

_____ I have to find a partner.

_____ I need to learn some basic phrases.

_____ I have to plan my trip.

_____ I need to buy some new shoes.

PROJECT **1**
Self-Improvement Plan

Make a poster showing something you want to improve about yourself and tell others about it.

A Discuss. Read about these people's plans to improve their lives. What advice do you have?

I'd like to make some new friends, so I'm thinking about joining a club. I guess that's the best way to meet new people.

I'd really like to lose some weight, so I'm thinking about going on a diet. I want to lose three kilograms this summer.

I'm always late for school because I can't wake up in the morning. I'm usually sleepy all day too. I'm going to go to bed earlier.

B Prepare. How would you like to improve yourself? Discuss ideas with a partner. Then choose your best idea and complete the chart.

What I want to do	How I will do it	How my life will improve
Stop being late for school	Go to bed before 11 p.m. Don't drink coffee at night	Get better grades Have more energy

C Create. Make a poster.

My Self-Improvement Plan

by Janice Lane

Stop being late for school

How I will do it
- ☑ Go to bed before 11 p.m.
- ☑ Don't drink coffee at night
- ☑ Get more exercise
- ☑ Don't go out in the evening on weekdays

How my life will improve
- ☺ Get better grades
- ☺ Be a better student
- ☺ Have more energy

Me before

Me after

D Speak. Tell your classmates about your self-improvement plan. Encourage each other and give advice.

Example:
A: I'd like to stop being late for school. I'm going to stop drinking coffee.

B: You should go to a fitness center.

C: That sounds great. Good luck!

Believe It or Not 4

Warm Up

Speak. Ask a partner about these personal experiences. What's the most interesting thing you found out?

Tell me about:
1. a trip you took.
2. a movie you saw.
3. a concert you went to.

Example:

A: Tell me about a trip you took.
B: I went to Thailand last year.
A: That sounds great.

Challenge Preview

A 🔘 **7** **Listen.** In the Challenge, some students are playing a truth-lie game. Who thinks Steven's story is true?

☐ Ethan

☐ Sang-mi

☐ Kirsten

Have you eaten anything strange?

Yes I have.

Let me tell you about it.

B 🔘 **7** **Write and listen again.** Fill in the missing past tense verbs to complete the story. Then listen to check your ideas.

| took   ate   was   ate   found   went |

Steven: Last summer, I _____ a trip to Canada. One day,
I _____ into a forest. I _____ an apple
and _____ it. But there _____ a bug
inside the apple, so I _____ that too!

Kirsten: Really?

Steven: Uh-huh. It was awful.

C **Speak.** Practice the conversation with a partner. Say **Really** like you believe Steven. Then practice the conversation again and say **Really** like you don't believe Steven.

Working on Language ▶ Telling a Story

What and Who	When	More Information	Opinion	
I went to a concert with my sister	two years ago. last week. when I was little.	We saw Madonna.	She was	amazing. great. terrible.

A Write. Make notes about two of your interesting experiences.

1

What and Who:

_____

_____

When:

_____

More Information:

_____

_____

Opinion:

_____

2

What and Who:

_____

_____

When:

_____

More Information:

_____

_____

Opinion:

_____

B Speak. Tell your stories to a partner.

Example:

A: Guess what. Last year, I went to an F1 race with my best friend. We saw a crash. It was horrible.

B: Really? That sounds scary.

Useful **Expressions**

Listen to this.
Guess what.
Let me tell you about . . .

Level Up!
See page 46.

Communicate ▸ Have You Ever?

A Speak. Take turns asking a partner about these experiences.
Answer with as much information as you can.

Example:

A: Have you ever gone camping?
B: No, I haven't. Have you?
A: Yes, I have. My family and I went camping
in England three years ago. I loved it.

ride a horse

go camping

make a snowman

have a pet

see a ghost

be on television

tell a lie

take music lessons

B Write and speak. Write new questions, using "Have you ever . . . ?"
Then ask some classmates your four questions.

1. _____

2. _____

3. _____

4. _____

Working on Fluency ▶ Showing Interest

A 🔘 **8** **Listen.** Yumi is telling a story about a homeless man.
Number the pictures from 1 to 4 in the order you hear them.

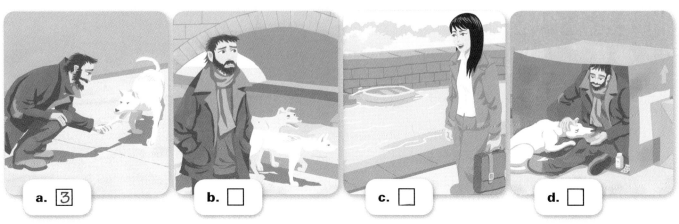

a. ⬚ 3 b. ☐ c. ☐ d. ☐

B 🔘 **8** **Listen again.** Which expressions does Luis use to show he is
interested in Yumi's story? Check [✓] them.

☐ OK.
☐ Uh-huh.
☐ Is that true?

☐ Oh, that sounds scary.
☐ Really?
☐ Oh, that's sad.

☐ That's really funny.
☐ That's a great story.
☐ I can't believe it.

C **Write and speak.** Complete the stories using your imagination. Then tell your
stories to a partner. The listener will use some expressions from activity B.

1. Guess what. When I was

   _____, I was in
   (when)
   _____.
   (a place)
   Suddenly, I saw _____.
   (famous person)
   (He/She) smiled at me and said "_____

   _____."

   I was so _____.
   (adjective)

2. Listen to this. Last night, I was on a bicycle ride

   with _____. It was dark.
   (person)
   Suddenly, I saw something

   _____ in the sky. It stopped
   (color)
   over my bicycle. Then, it flew away. I think it was

   _____.
   (a thing)

Challenge

Play the Truth-Lie Game. Make a group and tell each other interesting stories. Some stories will be true and others will be lies.

A Write. Think how you would answer these two questions. Write one true story and one lie. Don't tell anyone which story is true.

Example: Have you eaten anything strange?
Yes, I have. One day, I was really hungry in class so I put an eraser in my mouth. Then the teacher asked me a question. I swallowed it by mistake.

Critical Thinking

Think about how to spot a lie. What do people do or say when they tell a lie? List three things.

1 Have you eaten anything strange?
Yes, I have . . .

_____

_____

_____

_____

2 Have you ever seen a crime?
Yes, I have . . .

_____

_____

_____

_____

_____

Push One

Truth   Lie

B Play the game. Get into groups of four students. For each question, follow these instructions.

1. Ask each person the same question.

Have you eaten anything strange?

2. Storyteller: say "yes" and tell a true story or a lie.

Yes, I have. I ate an eraser once . . .

3. Listeners: push the Truth or Lie button.

4. Listeners: get one point for each correct guess. Write how many points you got.

Your Classmates' Names	1. Have you ever eaten anything strange?	2. Have you ever seen a crime?	3. Have you ever lost anything valuable?	4. Have you ever had an unusual friend?	5. Have you ever been really scared?
				TOTAL:	

Reflection Time

Write useful words and ideas you learned in this unit.

When You Have Time ▶ Extra Activities

If you finish an activity in this unit before your classmates, try one of these.

A Do the crossword puzzle.

Change I *find* to I have *found*.

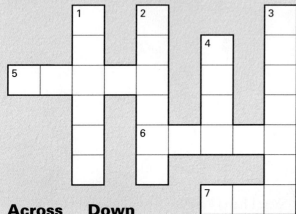

Across	Down
5. find	**1.** buy
6. eat	**2.** ride
7. have	**3.** learn
	4. lose

B Do the quiz. Where do these company names come from? Are they true or false?

1. Apple: from the company president's favorite fruit _____

2. SONY: from the first letters of four Japanese names _____

3. Hotmail: from HTML _____

4. Panasonic: because the company made pots and pans first _____

5. Disneyland: because the rides make you feel dizzy _____

6. Microsoft: from microcomputer software _____

7. CISCO: from San Francisco _____

C Talk with a partner about personal change.

1. What is one of your most important experiences?

2. When did it happen?

3. Did it change you? How?

4. Are you happy that it happened?

Level Up

Make your stories more interesting by using stronger adjectives.

Example:
But there was a bug inside the apple, so I ate that too. ▶ It was **awful**.
It was **disgusting**.

Complete these sentences with a partner. Then practice saying them with a partner. Be expressive!

> huge   deafening   starving
> terrified   hilarious

1. I saw a comedy show on TV last night. I laughed so much. It was _____.

2. I went to a rock concert last month. The band was really loud. They were _____.

3. I saw a ghost when I was little. I was _____.

4. The homeless man was _____ because he didn't have enough to eat.

5. I lost my cell phone about a month ago. This was a _____ problem for me.

Where I Grew Up 5

☐ a park

☐ a scary place

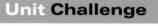

☐ a store you like

Unit Challenge

▸ Make a map of your hometown.
▸ Give your classmates a tour.

Warm Up

A Check [✓]. Which of these places do you have in your hometown?

B Speak. Tell a partner about some places in your hometown.

Example:
A: I'm from Springfield. There's a park near my house.
B: What's it like?
A: It's small. I sometimes played there with my best friends, Ryan and Andrew.

☐ a place you play sports

☐ a relative's house

Challenge Preview

A 🔘 **9** **Listen.** In the Challenge, Ethan and Ana are talking about their hometowns. What did Ana and her boyfriend used to talk about?

☐ the future
☐ the past
☐ their friends
☐ high school

> Let me give you a tour of my hometown.

B 🔘 **9** **Write and listen again.** Fill in the missing words that start these questions. Then listen to check your ideas.

> do   how often   why   what

Ana: Well, there was a **river** near my house. It was really **beautiful**.

Ethan: _____ is that place special for you?

Ana: I used to go there with my **boyfriend**.

Ethan: _____ did you go?

Ana: **Every day, usually**.

Ethan: That sounds nice. _____ did you do there?

Ana: We used to talk about our dreams and college— you know, the future.

Ethan: _____ you still go there?

Ana: Yes, sometimes.

C **Speak.** Practice the conversation with a partner. Then change the words in **red** to talk about this photo.

▶ coffee shop
▶ popular
▶ my friends
▶ about once a week

Working on Language ▶ Describing Past Routines

I **used to** go to the park **when** I was little.

When I was in high school, I **used to** play baseball.

A Write. Describe what you used to do when you were younger.

1. I used to play _____ , when I was little.

2. I used to _____ , when I was younger.

3. When I was in junior high school, I used to _____

4. When I was in elementary school, I used to love _____

B Speak. Tell a partner what you used to do. Your partner
will ask follow-up questions.

Example:
A: When I was little, I used to play soccer.
B: Oh really? Me too. Were you on the school team?
A: Yes, I was. I was a striker.

Useful Expressions
Oh, really?
Me too.
That sounds like fun.

Communicate ▶ What Happened?

A Write. Think of five interesting personal experiences and complete the chart. Use these ideas or others of your own.

find something unusual

get hurt in an accident

win a prize

do something bad with friends

go on a date

play a sport

When did it happen?	What happened?	Where did it happen?
eight years old	found an old box	park

B Speak. Tell a partner about your experiences. Your partner will ask follow-up questions.

A: When I was eight years old, I found something unusual.
It was an old silver box. I found it in the park.

B: Was there anything inside?

A: Yes, there was. There was a coin inside . . .

Working on Fluency ▶ Describing in Detail

A 🔘 **10** **Listen.** You are going to do a relaxation exercise. It will help you remember a place, or maybe a person, or an event. Close your eyes and listen.

B **Write.** Make notes on what you remembered: a person, a place, an event, a sound, a smell, etc.

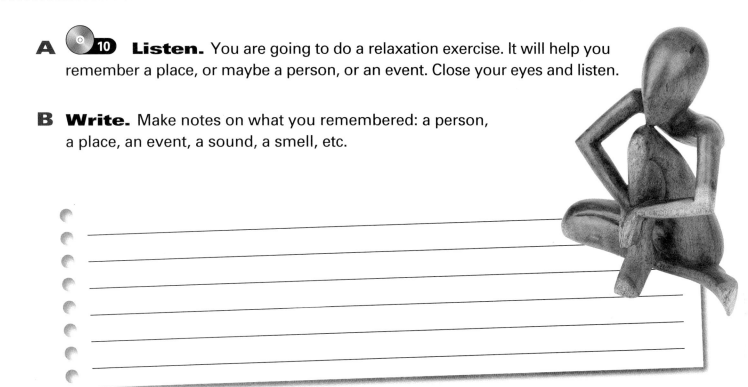

C **Speak.** Get into groups and talk about your experiences. Your classmates will ask these and other follow-up questions. Take turns.

Level Up!
See page 54.

Challenge

Make a map of your hometown and give your classmates a tour of some special places.

A Write. Think of four special places in your hometown and complete the chart. Use the example to help you.

Where is the special place?	Why is it special?
Tower Movie Theater	I went on my first date there when I was 16.

💡 Critical Thinking

Think about how to make your hometown tour more interesting. Write the most interesting thing you can say about each place.

B Prepare. Make a simple map of your hometown and label your four special places.

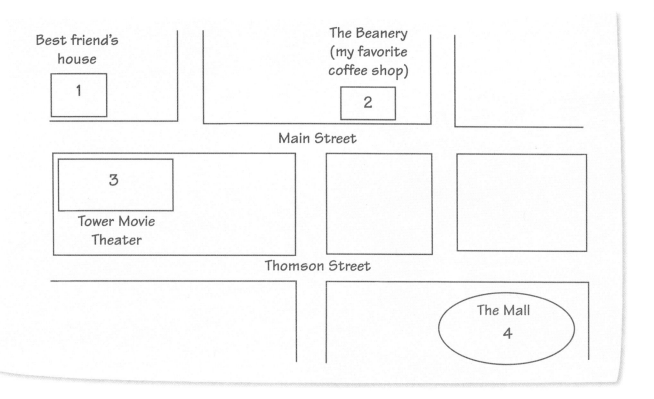

Best friend's house

1

The Beanery (my favorite coffee shop)

2

Main Street

3

Tower Movie Theater

Thomson Street

The Mall

4

C Speak. Tell other students about your special places. Your partners will ask follow-up questions.

Example:

A: Tell me about a special place in your hometown.

B: Well, I used to go to the Tower Movie Theater when I was in high school.

A: What's special about that place for you?

B: I had my first date there when I was 16 . . .

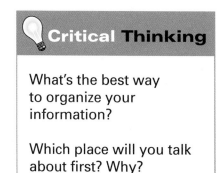

Critical Thinking

What's the best way to organize your information?

Which place will you talk about first? Why?

Reflection Time

Write useful words and ideas you learned in this unit.

When You Have Time ▶ Extra Activities

If you finish an activity in this unit before your classmates, try one of these.

A Match the words and pictures.

_____ stadium   _____ art museum

_____ Buddhist temple _____ church

_____ cemetery   _____ swimming pool

B Write the words from activity A in the lists below. Some of the places fit in more than one list. Add one more of your own to each list:

Scary Places:

Cultural Places:

Religious Places:

Sports Facilities:

C Talk with a partner about where you grew up.

1. What's your favorite restaurant in your hometown?
2. Where did you used to go after school?
3. What do you remember most from your hometown?
4. Where did you usually go for fun with your family?

Level Up

Make your stories more interesting by using stronger adjectives.
Put these adjectives into the correct category.

> huge   noisy   calm   quiet   minute
> salty   devastated   delicious   spicy
> delighted   colorful   deafening

Sounds

_____ _____ _____

Tastes

_____ _____ _____

Sights

_____ _____ _____

Feelings

_____ _____ _____

Now write sentences for each category.

Example: I heard the sound of the train.
It was _deafening._

1. I heard the sound of _____
2. I saw _____
3. I smelled _____
4. When I saw her smile, I felt

_____

Bargain Shopper 6

from an online auction site

at a night market

at a vintage clothing shop

1950s Fashion

at a flea market

at a clearance sale

Warm Up

Speak. Ask a partner about shopping at these places.

Example:
A: Have you ever bought something at a night market?
B: Sure. I bought some souvenirs at a night market in Taipei.
A: When was that?
B: Last year.

Challenge Preview

A 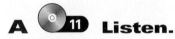 **Listen.**

In the Challenge, Sang-mi and Steven are doing a shopping role-play. How much does Steven pay for the watch?

- ☐ $200
- ☐ $180
- ☐ $150
- ☐ $145

Hello. May I help you?

Yes, please. Can you tell me about this watch?

Time Flies

B 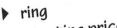 **Write and listen again.** Fill in the missing adjectives to complete the conversation. Then listen to check your ideas.

> real   reasonable   popular   beautiful

Sang-mi: This **watch** is _____ gold. It's _____, isn't it?

Steven: Yes, it is.

Sang-mi: It's a very _____ brand. And it's a _____ price too.

Steven: Really? How much is it?

Sang-mi: It's **$200**.

Steven: That's too much. Can you give me a better price?

Sang-mi: OK. I can let you have it for **$180**.

C **Speak.** Practice the conversation with a partner. Then change the words in **red** to talk about this photo.

- ▸ ring
- ▸ starting price = $50
- ▸ final price = $45

Working on Language ▶ Describing Items

	Adjective and Noun	More Information	Question
This is a	leather briefcase. handmade necklace.	**It's** from France. **It's** 100% silver.	It's nice, isn't it? Do you like it?

A Write. Complete these descriptions. Use the words below or your own ideas.

gold	silver	designer	popular	beautiful	cute
silk	leather	handmade	high quality	fashionable	cool

1. This is a _____ digital camera.
It's a really _____ model. _____

2. _____
_____

3. _____
_____

4. _____
_____

Your Idea:

5. _____
_____

B Speak. Describe the items above to a partner. Your partner will agree or disagree with you.

Example:

A: This is a high-quality digital camera. It's from Germany.
It's nice, isn't it?
B: Sorry. It's a little old-fashioned.

Useful Expressions

I love it!
Sorry. It's not my taste.
Sorry. It's a little old-fashioned.

Communicate ▶ May I Help You?

A Write. Complete this conversation using the sentences in the box below.

> OK. Thanks. I'll take it.   Can you tell me about this camera?
>
> That's still too much. How about $50? That's too expensive. Can you give me a better price?

Seller: Hello. May I help you?

Shopper: _____

Seller: Sure. It's a brand new, high-quality camera. It's only $80.

Shopper: _____

Seller: I can let you have it for $70.

Shopper: _____

Seller: No, but I'll let you have it for $60.

Shopper: _____

B Speak. Put some personal items on your desk. Take turns with a partner to sell them in your own currency. Take notes.

Level Up! See page 62.

I bought a . . .	for
pen	$ 4

I sold a . . .	for
ruler	$ 1

Working on Fluency ▶ Refusing an Offer

A 💿 **12** **Listen.** Bargaining expert Rick Jeeves is shopping for a camera. Number Rick's bargaining tips in order from 1 to 6. Then listen to check your ideas.

_____ Ask for a lower price.   _____ Walk away.

_____ Ask about the item you want.   _____ Offer a really low price.

_____ Compare prices.   _____ Accept the offer.

B 💿 **12** **Listen again.** How does Rick refuse the seller's offers? Check [✓] the expressions you hear.

☐ No, thanks. I'm just looking.   ☐ Thanks, but that's too much.

☐ That's high.   ☐ I don't think so.

☐ No way!   ☐ No, sorry.

☐ I'm afraid not.

C **Speak.** Take turns selling these things to a partner. Bargain over the price.

> 💡 **Critical Thinking**
>
> Think about how to refuse something politely. Circle three polite responses in activity B. Then decide which response is the least polite.

$25

$200

$300

$40

Example:

A: This backpack is really cool. It's $300. Would you like to buy it?

B: Sorry. That's too high.

A: How about $200?

B: I'm afraid not.

A: OK. I can let you have it for $60.

B: Thanks. I'll take it.

Challenge

This is a shopping role-play. Some students are sellers trying to make a profit and other students are shoppers trying to save money.

A **Read.** Look at the price guide to help you buy and sell your bags, watches, and cameras.

Price Guide
Maximum prices are:
$100 for all high-quality items
$50 for all good-value items
$20 for all discount items

B **Read.** Get into two groups, shoppers and sellers. There should be roughly one seller for every three shoppers. Shoppers: read the shopper instructions below. Sellers: read the seller instructions on the next page.

SHOPPERS

1. You have $200. Buy three items: one bag, one watch, and one camera. One item must be high-quality, another "good value for money," and another must be a cheaper discount item.

2. Try to spend as little as possible. Fill in the chart.

	Item	Price
High Quality	watch	$43
Good Value		
Discount		
	Total Cost:	

SELLERS

1. Make a bag, watch, or camera store. Draw one high-quality item, one "good value for money" item, and one cheap discount item. Decide a starting price for each item. (The starting price must be higher than your cost—see chart below.)

2. Bargain with shoppers. Try to sell at high prices.

Item	Sold to	Sale price	Item cost (starting price)	Profit
High quality bag	Luis	$42	$20	$22

3. When you sell something, fill in the chart. Then calculate your profit. (Sale price – item cost = profit.)

C Role play. After the shops are set up, bargain for goods. At the end, decide who the best shoppers and sellers are.

Can you tell me about your best value bag?

The *Bag Lady*

When You Have Time ▶ Extra Activities

If you finish an activity in this unit before your classmates, try one of these.

A Do the shopaholic survey. Write T (true) or F (false).

	True	False
I shop more than once a week.		
I always buy something when I shop.		
I sometimes hide what I buy.		
I know some salespeople's names.		
I buy new clothes for every party.		
When I feel sad, shopping makes me feel better.		
I sometimes don't eat to save money for shopping.		

If you have more than five Ts, see a doctor soon!

B In what stores do you buy these items? The same stores in the U.S. and the U.K. have different names.

U.S. Stores
men's store
candy store
grocery store
stationery store
drugstore

U.K. Stores
greengrocer's
chemist's
tailor's
stationer's
confectioner's

Item	U.S. Stores
medicine	_____
chocolates	_____
envelopes	_____
tomatoes	_____
a man's suit	_____

	U.K. Stores
medicine	_____
chocolates	_____
envelopes	_____
tomatoes	_____
a man's suit	_____

C Talk about your favorite stores with a partner.

1. What's your favorite store?
2. What have you bought there?
3. Why do you like it?
4. How can I get there?

Level Up

Here are some other bargaining expressions. Put the conversation in order. Then practice with a partner

____ No thanks, I'm just looking.

_1_ Do you need any help?

____ Thanks, it's a deal.

____ It's $45.

____ Yes, it's nice. How much are you asking for it?

____ I only have $40.

____ You're welcome.

____ Well, OK, I can sell it to you for $40.

____ How about this watch? Do you like it?

PROJECT **2**

Flea Market

Bring four items from home that you want to sell. Hold a class flea market and sell them.

A Discuss. Some people are selling their things at a flea market. Read the sales tag for each item. Would you buy them? Why or why not?

Check this out! It's an official Boston Red Sox baseball cap. It's very cool, isn't it? It costs $35 new—only $10.

Hungry? These homemade cookies are really delicious—just like grandma used to make. Three cookies for a dollar.

Games! Games! Games! This retro video game console is a lot of fun. It's old, but it still works perfectly. It's cheap—only $15.

B Prepare. What could you sell at a class flea market? Write at least four ideas.

What you want to sell	Good things about it	Price
baseball cap	– official baseball cap – very cool – originally $35	$10.00

C Create. Write a sales tag for each item you are going to sell.

D Make a shop. Set up a shop with a partner. Put your sale items and sales tags on a desk.

E Buy and sell. Sell your items while your partner goes shopping. Take turns.

Example:

A: What's this?

B: It's a video game.

A: Really? When did you get it?

B: A while ago. It still works. I used to play it a lot.

A: How much is it?

B: It's cheap—only $15.

A: $15? Can you give me a better price? . . .

The Perfect Gift

Unit Challenge

▸ Think of a great gift to give someone.
▸ Explain your gift to some classmates.

Warm Up

A Check [✓]. On which of these occasions have you given a gift?

☐ to say "sorry" to someone
☐ to a couple on their wedding day
☐ to your mom on Mother's Day
☐ to someone special on Valentine's Day
☐ to someone after you came back from a trip
☐ to someone in the hospital

B Speak. Compare your answers with a partner.

Example:
A: Have you ever given a gift to say "sorry" to someone?
B: Yes, I have.
A: What did you give?
B: A box of chocolates.

Challenge Preview

A  **🔵 13 Listen.** Ana is explaining her gift idea to Yumi. Why would Ana like to give her friend a gift?

☐ Emma's dream is to go to the United States.

☐ Emma helped Ana.

☐ Emma's father lives in the United States.

What's your gift?

I have the perfect gift for my friend.

B **🔵 13 Write and listen again.** Fill in the missing words. Then listen to check your ideas.

> scholarship   study trip   high school   study abroad

Ana: I'd like to give Emma a one-year _____ to the United States.

Yumi: Uh-huh.

Ana: Her school gave her a _____ when she was in _____ but she couldn't go.

Yumi: Really?

Ana: Yes, her father got sick, so she had to take care of him.

Yumi: That's too bad.

Ana: Emma really wanted to _____, and it's still her dream. So, I want to give her that chance.

Yumi: That's a lovely gift, Ana.

C **Speak.** Practice the conversation with a partner. Then change the words in **red** and practice more ways of showing interest.

▸ Oh, that's sad.
▸ No way!
▸ Is that true?

Working on Language ▶ Explaining Gift Ideas

	What		**Why**
I would like	to give Ana a gift	**because**	she's a good friend. she's teaching me Spanish. she helped my brother find a job.

A **Write.** Think of five gifts you would like to give and why you would like to give them. Use the ideas below to get started.

buy lunch for my friend
invited me to her party

take my dad to a baseball game
always works so hard

1. I would like to _____.

2. _____

3. Your idea (a family member): _____

4. Your idea (a friend): _____

5. Your idea: _____

B **Speak.** Share your ideas with a partner.

Example:

A: I'd like to take my dad to a baseball game, because he works so hard.

B: That's very thoughtful of you.

> **Useful Expressions**
>
> You're so kind.
> That's very thoughtful of you.
> That's nice of you.

Communicate ▸ Thank You!

A Speak. Thank your partner for three of the things below.

Example:
A: I'd like to thank you for reminding me about the homework.
B: You're welcome.

remind me about the homework

give me advice

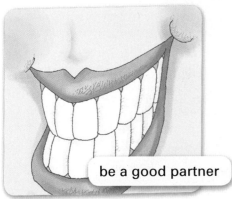

be a good partner

help me with English

lend me a pencil

share your textbook with me

give me something to eat

Your Idea!

B Speak. Choose a student to thank for something. That student will thank another student, and so on.

Kirsten, I'd like to thank you for showing me how to buy a train ticket.

Yumi, I'd like to thank you for doing my homework.

Ssshhh!

Working on Fluency ▶ Giving and Receiving

A 🔘 **14** **Listen.** Ethan is giving Kirsten a ring. Listen to the conversations and check [✓] the statements you think are correct.

1. Kirsten and Ethan are:

☐ friends.

☐ boyfriend and girlfriend.

2. Ethan gave Kirsten:

☐ a large gift.

☐ a very special gift.

3. Kirsten likes the ring because:

☐ it's beautiful.

☐ it means Ethan is her boyfriend now.

B **Write.** Use these sentences to complete the conversation.

> Do you like it?   Thank you so much.
> You're welcome.   Can I open it?

💡 **Critical Thinking**

Think about the situation in activity A. What do you think Kirsten should say to Ethan?

Ethan: I have a present for you.

Kirsten: For me? You shouldn't have. _____

Ethan: Yes, of course. Please do.

Kirsten: Oh, it's a ring.

Ethan: _____

Kirsten: Yes, it's beautiful. _____

Ethan: _____

Level Up!
See page 72.

C **Speak.** Take turns giving these gifts to a partner. Use the conversation above.

Your Idea!

Challenge

Think of a perfect gift for someone special in your life and tell your classmates about it. The gift can be anything, even something impossible.

A Read and check [✓]. Read about one student's gift and check the reason for giving it.

- ☐ The new house is far away.
- ☐ The student's brother is very kind.
- ☐ The student thinks babies are noisy.
- ☐ The student thinks the house is too small.

Who
my brother and his wife

What and Why
My brother and his wife still live at home with my parents and me. Our house is really small and noisy.

Guess what? My brother's wife is going to have a baby in a few months.

I'd like to give my brother and sister-in-law their own house, because they need more space.

B Write. Think of the gift you want to give and ask yourself:

- ▶ Who do you want to give a gift to?
- ▶ What would you like to give?
- ▶ Why would you like to give it?

C Speak. Tell your classmates about your gift. They will ask you questions about it.

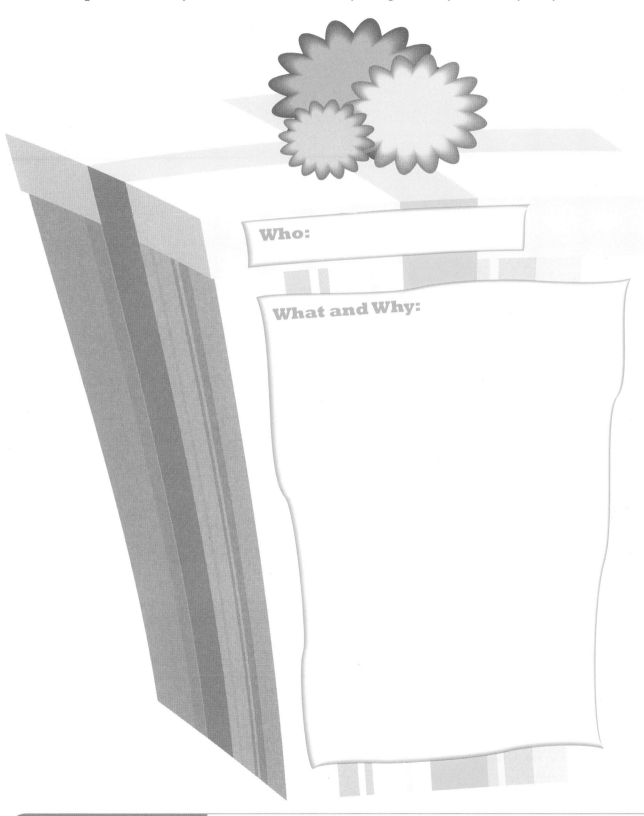

Who:

What and Why:

Reflection Time

Write useful words and ideas you learned in this unit.

When You Have Time ▶ Extra Activities

If you finish an activity in this unit before your classmates, try one of these.

A Do the crossword puzzle.

Across

3. I gave him chocolate on _____ Day.

4. Thanks for the gift. It's _____!

6. You're _____ kind.

7. I gave a rose to my mom on _____ Day.

8. That's very thoughtful _____ you.

Down

1. I would like to thank you for _____ me a cookie.

2. I am going to give her a cat _____ she is lonely.

5. What's your _____ for giving him this gift?

B Think of kind things you can do for someone.

The second week of February is Random Acts of Kindness Week in the United States. Read these examples of gifts you can give strangers. Then think of your own.

▶ Buy dessert for a stranger as you leave a restaurant.

▶ Take a neighbor's dog for a walk.

▶ Pay the road fare for the car behind you too.

▶ Pick up litter as you walk home.

C Talk with a partner about gift giving.

1. What is the best gift you ever received?

2. Who gave it to you? Why?

3. Why do you like it so much?

4. Do you still have it?

Level Up

Here are some other ways for thanking, and responding to thanks. Complete the conversation. Then practice with a partner.

> very grateful   appreciate it   say thanks
> no problem   mention it

A: I just want to _____ for looking after my cat while I was away.

B: Oh, it was _____.

A: Really, I'm _____. It was a great help.

B: That's OK. Any time.

A: Well, I'm glad it was no problem. I really _____.

B: Sure. Don't _____.

Party Planner

New Year's party

birthday party

barbecue

all-night party

Warm Up

A Check [✓]. Which of these parties have you gone to?

B Speak. Think of a party you went to and tell a partner about it.

Example:

A: When I was a child, I went to a birthday party in a park. I'll never forget it.

B: Why? What did you do?

A: My friends and I rode horses. It was a great day.

wedding

Challenge Preview

A  **15 Listen.**

Sang-mi is inviting Luis to a barbecue. Who else is she going to invite?

- ☐ her classmates
- ☐ her English teacher
- ☐ her family

> We're having a barbecue on Saturday. Can you come?

> Saturday? I'm a little busy this weekend.

B **15 Write and listen again.** Fill in the missing *Wh-* question words. Then listen and check your ideas.

> what else   what time   what   who

Luis: _____'s going to come?

Sang-mi: I'm inviting everyone from our English class.

Luis: So _____ are you going to do?

Sang-mi: Well, we're going to **cook some burgers and hot dogs**.

Luis: _____ are you going to do?

Sang-mi: **Yumi's band is going to play for us** too.

Luis: Hey, that sounds fun. _____ does it start?

Sang-mi: At about **7:30**. So you can come?

Luis: Sure, I'd love to.

C Speak. Practice the conversation with a partner. Then change the words in **red** to talk about this photo.

Halloween party
▸ wear costumes
▸ dance all night.
▸ 9:30

Working on Language ▶ Asking for Information

Use **going to** to ask questions about future events.	Where are we **going to** eat dinner?
Use **should** to ask for a suggestion.	**Should** I bring my camera?

A Write. Imagine you are invited to a class picnic. Think of questions you could ask, using "going to," and "should." Use the example below to help you.

1. Where: _Where are you going to have the picnic?_____

2. When: _____

3. Who: _____

4. Something to drink: _____

5. What to do: _____

6. What to eat: _____

7. Something to eat: _____

8. How much: _____

B Write. Imagine someone is inviting you to these events. Think of a question you could ask about each event.

Level Up!
See page 80.

1. I'm going to a movie tonight. Do you want to come?

2. My sister is getting married this weekend. Please come.

3. We're going on a hike on Monday. Can you come?

_____   _____   _____

_____   _____   _____

C Speak. Invite a partner to the three events above. Your partner will ask you follow-up questions about them.

Example:
A: I'm going to a movie tonight. Do you want to come?
B: Maybe. Where should we meet?
A: At the Grand Theater . . .

Communicate ▶ I'd love to come!

I'm going to the library tonight. Do you want to come?	**Accept:** Yes, I'd love to. **Not sure:** I'm not sure I can. I'll check my schedule and tell you later. **Refuse:** I'm sorry. I can't. I'm busy.

Speak. Invite a partner to four of these events. Remember to say when you are going. Your partner will ask questions, and then accept or refuse your invitation.

Example:

A: Please come to my house for a study meeting tonight.

B: What are we going to study?

A: Grammar.

B: Oh, I'm sorry. I can't. I have to clean my room.

on a hike

on a bug hunt

to a dance

to my sister's pot-luck dinner party

to a class picnic

to a beach party

to a wedding

to the library

Your idea!

Working on Fluency ▶ Responding to Suggestions

A 🔘 **16** **Listen.** Some people are planning four different parties. Number the parties in order from 1 to 4.

a. ☐ Halloween party **b.** ☐ all-night party **c.** ☐ wedding **d.** ☐ surprise party

B 🔘 **16** **Listen again.** Now listen to each suggestion, and circle the answer you hear.

1. Let's surprise her when she gets home.

Yeah, I like it. / Well, I'm not sure.

2. Let's make them feed the cake to each other?

That sounds fun. / That's a good idea.

3. How about this? Let's dress up together in a horse costume.

How about this instead? / Yeah, I like it.

4. Let's get some DVDs, make popcorn, and watch movies all night.

That's a good idea. / Well, I'm not sure.

> **💡 Critical Thinking**
>
> Think about the responses in activity B. Which ones mean the speaker agrees? Which ones mean the speaker disagrees? Write "A" for agree or "X" for disagree.

C **Speak.** Work with a partner. Plan a birthday party for someone in your class. Use the expressions in activity B and make notes.

1. Before the party:

_____

_____

2. When the party starts:

_____

_____

3. Next:

_____

_____

4. Finally:

_____

_____

Example:

A: Let's make a cake together before the party.

B: Oh, that's a great idea. Let's bake a chocolate cake.

A: Well, I'm not sure. She doesn't like chocolate.

Challenge

Plan a party with a partner and invite your classmates. Then the class will choose the most interesting parties.

A Discuss and write. Work with a partner. Think of an original party idea and make a plan for it. Write all the things you will do at the party.

Example: Let's do this at the cooking party. Everyone will cook an original dish.

Notes:

_____

_____

_____

_____

_____

_____

B Prepare. Make an invitation on a piece of paper.

Come to our
Cooking Party!

Details:
When: Sunday, May 21
Time: from 3 p.m. to 7 p.m.
Where: Luis' house
Cost: $6.00 for ingredients
What to bring: a frying pan, pot, big spoon, and other cooking things
RSVP

Party Plan:
3 p.m.: we explain the contest
3 to 5 p.m.: each group makes an original dish
5 p.m.: we eat
6 p.m.: we vote on the best dish

C Speak. Follow these instructions.

Partners: Steven and Sang-mi

Partner A: Steven

Partner B: Sang-mi

1. Partner A invites students to the party.

2. Partner B walks around the room and:
   – gets invitations.
   – asks questions.
   – accepts/refuses invitations.

3. Partners A and B discuss the invitations and choose the three most interesting parties.

What kind of party is it?

Hi, please come to my party tomorrow. It will be fun.

You are invited to the COOKING PARTY

After a while, the teacher will ask you and your partner to change roles.

D Speak. Have a class vote on the most interesting parties.

Reflection Time

Write useful words and ideas you learned in this unit.

When You Have Time ▶ Extra Activities

If you finish an activity in this unit before your classmates, try one of these.

A Do the crossword puzzle.

Across

1. _____ party: white and black
4. _____ party: I'm 21 today!
6. _____ party: in December
7. _____ party: with coworkers

Down

2. _____ party: the last day of school
3. _____ party: turn the lights off and hide
4. _____ party: near the ocean
5. _____ : eat outside

B Talk with a partner about family events.

1. Does your family celebrate Christmas?
2. What other events does your family celebrate?
3. Which do you like best?
4. What do you do for (event)?

C Write the name of one country for each birthday tradition: Ireland, Denmark, Korea, Mexico.

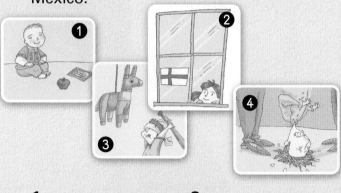

1. _____ 2. _____
3. _____ 4. _____

Level Up

You can use "will" to talk about future events. Look at this party invitation.

> ### Come to the International Society End of Term Party!
>
> **When:** Saturday, July 2, from 8:30 p.m.
> **Where:** Club Code
> **Cost:** $20 (price includes one drink, food, and entertainment)

Now write questions to complete each exchange.

Example: Who will come to the party?
Students from the International Society.

1. _____
   At 8:30 p.m.

2. _____
   At Club Code.

3. _____
   $20.

4. _____
   Some snacks.

5. Your question and answer:
   _____
   _____

Music Profile

Unit Challenge

▸ Interview a classmate.
▸ Make a music profile.
▸ Do a presentation.

Warm Up

A Write. Rank the kinds of music you like from 1 (the most) to 6 (the least).

☐ soul   ☐ rock music   ☐ pop music

☐ classical music   ☐ Latin music   ☐ hip-hop

B Speak. Ask your classmates about their tastes in music.

Example:

A: Do you like soul?

B: Yes, I do. How about you?

A: No, not really. Do you like rock?

B: No, I don't, but I really like pop music.

Challenge Preview

A 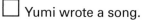 **Listen.** Sang-mi is telling the class about Yumi's taste in music. What's the most interesting thing Sang-mi learned?

☐ Yumi would like to be a DJ.

☐ Yumi loves to dance.

☐ Yumi wrote a song.

I interviewed Yumi about her musical tastes.

B 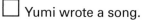 **Write and listen again.** Fill in the missing words. Then listen to check your ideas.

> loves   crazy   into   favorite

Sang-mi: **Yumi** said she _____ all kinds of music and listens to it all the time. **Yumi** is really

_____ **hip-hop**, and she is _____ about the group **"Black Eyed Peas."**

"Where is the Love?" is one of her _____ songs, and it reminds her of her **high school.**

Yumi saw **"Black Eyed Peas"** in concert last year. She said they were amazing.

C **Speak.** Practice the presentation with a partner. Then change the words in **red** to talk about this group.

- Sang-mi
- Likes rock music.
- Favorite group: Linkin Park
- Favorite song: Breaking the Habit
- Reminds her: her boyfriend

Working on Language ▶ Asking Questions

A **Write.** Complete the questions and answers using the words below.

Who's your	What do you	I love hip-hop.	She has a great voice.
Why do you	Do you ever	Yes, I have.	Sometimes.
Have you ever	Can you	Sure.	Alicia Keys.
What kind of	Do you	I like them a lot.	Just the piano.

1. _____ music are you into?   _____

2. _____ been to a rock concert?   _____

3. _____ think of U2?   _____

4. _____ like BoA?   _____

5. _____ listen to classical music?   _____

6. _____ favorite singer?   _____

7. _____ like her?   _____

8. _____ play a musical instrument?   _____

B **Speak.** Ask a partner the questions above. Your partner will answer with real information.

Example:
A: What kind of music are you into?
B: I love R&B.
A: Really? Who's your favorite artist?
B: I'm crazy about the Japanese singer, Utada Hikaru. She's really talented.

Useful Expressions

She's really talented.
He has a great voice.
She's really creative.

Communicate ▶ Do You Live for Music?

A **Write.** Use these ideas to write five questions for a music survey. Then write your own answer for each one.

your musical abilities?

your favorites?

your recommendations?

where you get music?

Your questions	Your answers	Partner 1	Partner 2	Partner 3
1. What's good to listen to when you feel down?	Beyoncé		✔	✗
2.				
3.				
4.				
5.				

B **Speak.** Now ask three students your questions. Are your musical tastes similar? Check [✔] the answers that are similar to yours.

Example:

A: What's good to listen to when you feel down?

B: I recommend Beyoncé. Her music really makes me feel good.

A: OK. Thanks.

Working on Fluency ▶ Reporting What Others Say

A 🔘 **18** **Listen.** The singer Lamon Ota is being interviewed. What did Ota tell the interviewer? Circle True or False.

1. He said he loves pop music.   True   False

2. He said he likes rock.   True   False

3. He told her his parents were into punk.   True   False

4. He said "The Ramones" were from London.   True   False

B **Write.** Change these interview questions and answers to reported speech.

> I like reggae.
> ▶ **He said (that)** he likes reggae.
> ▶ **He told her (that)** he likes reggae.

Critical Thinking

Think about other questions the interviewer might ask Lamon. What three questions would give the most information about Lamon's band? Write them.

1. I really like punk.
   He told her _____

2. You should listen to "The Ramones."
   He said she _____

3. I recommend "Blitzkrieg Bop."
   He told _____

4. I love the lyrics.
   He said _____

C **Speak.** Get into groups of three. One person asks questions, the second person whispers the answers to the third person. Then the third person "reports" the answers.

Level Up!
See page 88.

What kind of music do you like?

I like classical music.

Kirsten said she likes classical music.

Challenge

Ask a partner questions about music and fill in the Music Profile. Then tell your classmates what you learned.

A **Write.** Look at the worksheet on the next page. Prepare your own questions for item 2 to 9.

1. What kind of music are you into? _____
2. _____
3. _____
4. _____
5. _____
6. _____

Other interesting questions about music:

7. _____
8. _____
9. _____
10. Is there anything else you'd like to tell me? _____

B **Speak.** Interview a partner and complete your worksheet.

C **Present.** Tell other students about your partner. Your classmates will ask you questions.

I interviewed Luis about music . . . The most interesting thing I learned about Luis is . . . he plays the drums in a rock band! . . . He told me he loves Elvis and The Beatles, . . . so they probably play classic rock songs.

Presentation Tip

Put pauses (. . .) before and after important points to make them stand out.

Reflection Time

Write useful words and ideas you learned in this unit.

(Name) _____'s

ROCKIN' MUSIC PROFILE

1. Favorite kind of music:

_____

2. Favorite singer or band:

_____

3. What he/she thinks of _____ :

_____

4. Best concert:

_____

5. Favorite song:

_____

6. Why he/she likes it:

_____

Other information

7. _____

_____

8. _____

_____

9. _____

_____

10. _____

_____

Comment

The most interesting thing I learned about (name) _____

is . . .

Optional Activity: Photocopy the completed worksheets and make a book. Make copies for everyone in the class.

When You Have Time ▶ Extra Activities

If you finish an activity in this unit before your classmates, try one of these.

A Do the instruments crossword puzzle.

Across
2. Strings and wood
4. Brass horn
5. Many keys
6. Jazz horn
7. Beat it

Down
1. Four or six strings
3. Electronic piano
4. Huge

B Music Quiz. Write the famous names in the correct list. Add one more famous person to each list.

> Ayumi Hamasaki   Avril Lavigne
> Bob Marley   Beyoncé
> John Coltrane   Shakira

Soul / R&B _____   Reggae _____

Jazz _____   Pop _____

Rock _____   Latin _____

C Talk with a partner about concerts.
1. Tell me about a concert you went to.
2. Where was it?
3. Whose concert would you like to go to?
4. Have you ever been *in* a concert?

Level Up

You can explain what questions you asked using "I asked . . ."

Example:
What kind of music do you like?
▶ **I asked what** kind of music he likes.

Do you like pop music?
▶ **I asked if** he likes pop music.

Put these questions into reported speech.

1. Are you into rock music?
   I asked if he _____

2. Which group do you recommend?
   I asked which _____

3. Are "The Ramones" a punk band?
   _____

4. What is their best song?
   _____

5. Why do you recommend that song?
   _____

Radio DJ

Be a DJ! Do a radio broadcast introducing your favorite song to your classmates.

A Discuss. This DJ is introducing her favorite songs. Imagine you are a DJ.
What song would you like to play?

Hey everybody! I'm DJ Maxine. Today, I'm going to play one of my favorite songs. It's called "Girlfriend" and it's by Avril Lavigne. It was a massive hit around the world, and was her first number-one single in the U.S. "Girlfriend" always makes me smile when I hear it. This is a great song. Turn up the volume and enjoy!

B Prepare. Choose a song you would like to introduce to your classmates.
Then find out some interesting information about the singer or band.
Complete the chart.

Name of song:	
Singer or band:	
Why do you like it?	
Kind of music:	
Nationality:	
Hit songs:	
Other info:	

C Create. Follow these instructions:

1. Fill in the blanks to complete the DJ script. Then practice.
2. Record the broadcast along with your song and prepare for a live broadcast.

☐ Hi, everybody!

☐ Hi, everyone!

☐ Yo! What's up?   I'm DJ (your name) _____.

Today, I'd like to play one of my favorite songs.

It's called (song title) _____ and it's by

(singer or band) _____.

(Write a sentence or two about the singer or band)

_____

_____

(Write a sentence or two about why you like this song)

_____

_____

(Choose one of these sentences to finish your script or write one of your own.)

☐   I really hope you'll like this song too. Check it out!

☐   This is a great song. Turn up the volume and enjoy!

☐   I love this song. I hope you will, too.

☐   _____

D Present. Play your DJ broadcast or read out your DJ script in class. Who's the best DJ?

Style Makeover

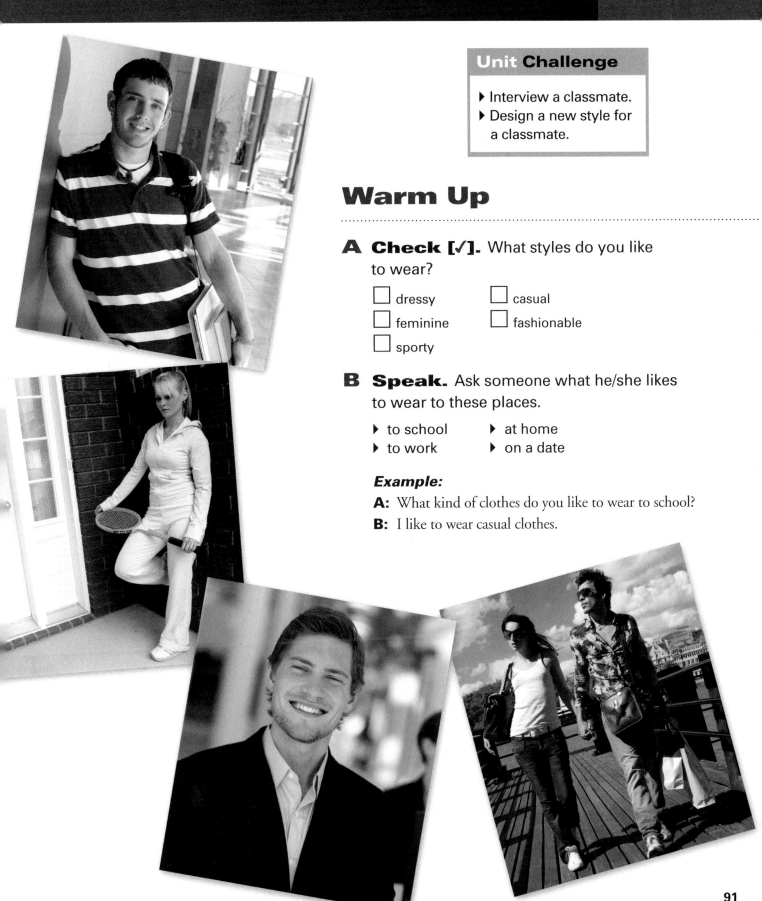

Unit Challenge

▸ Interview a classmate.
▸ Design a new style for a classmate.

Warm Up

A Check [✓]. What styles do you like to wear?

- ☐ dressy
- ☐ feminine
- ☐ sporty
- ☐ casual
- ☐ fashionable

B Speak. Ask someone what he/she likes to wear to these places.

- ▸ to school
- ▸ to work
- ▸ at home
- ▸ on a date

Example:

A: What kind of clothes do you like to wear to school?
B: I like to wear casual clothes.

Challenge Preview

A 🔊 **19** **Listen.** Steven is giving a presentation about Ethan's "style makeover." How does Steven describe Ethan's new style?

- ☐ sporty
- ☐ unusual
- ☐ dressy
- ☐ feminine
- ☐ fashionable
- ☐ casual

> Hi, everybody. I'm Steven—Ethan's stylist.

CURRENT STYLE   NEW STYLE

B 🔊 **19** **Write and listen again.** Fill in the missing words to describe Ethan's current style. Then listen to check your ideas.

> white leather   brown cotton   blue denim

Steven: Today, I'm going to tell you about Ethan's "style makeover." This is Ethan's "**current look.**" Ethan is wearing _____ **pants** and a _____ **shirt**. He's also wearing some _____ **sneakers**. It's a very **casual look.**

C **Speak.** Practice the conversation with a partner. Then change the words in **red** to talk about Ethan's "new look."

Ethan's "new look"
- ▸ black denim jeans
- ▸ black leather vest
- ▸ brown leather cowboy boots
- ▸ fashionable look

Working on Language ▶ Describing Clothes

	Color(s)	Design or Material	Clothing item
She's wearing	a blue and white	checked	dress.
He's wearing	white	leather	sneakers.

A Write. Label the clothes pictures using the words below to help you.

> cotton   leather   denim
> wool   striped   checked
> short/long-sleeved

> T-shirt   polo shirt   blouse   sweater
> pants   skirt   shorts   dress
> sandals   high heels   sneakers

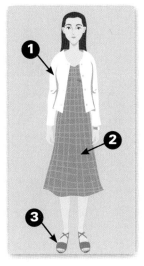
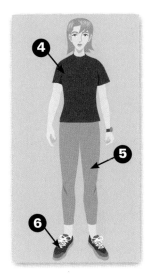
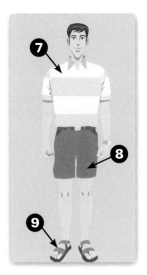

1. _a white wool sweater_

2. _a red checked dress_

3. _brown leather sandals_

4. _____

5. _____

6. _____

7. _____

8. _____

9. _____

10. _____

11. _____

12. _____

B Ask. Are there any other clothes words you would like to know the English for? Ask your teacher, or use a dictionary, and write them down.

Level Up!
See page 98.

C Speak. Look what your partner is wearing today. Then sit or stand back-to-back and say what your partner is wearing. Can you remember?

Example:
A: You're wearing a red and white checked shirt, black jeans, and sneakers.
B: No, not exactly. I'm wearing dark blue jeans.

Communicate ▶ Find Her!

A Speak. Your partner will choose someone below. Ask your partner *yes/no* questions to find out who it is. Ask as few questions as possible.

Example:

A: Is she wearing a T-shirt?

B: Yes.

A: Is she wearing blue?

B: No.

A: Is she wearing sandals?

B: No.

A: It's Jan.

Jan Lynn Jill Sue Alex Kate

Liz Maria Kim Andrea Paula Joan

Hannah Ann Jane Keiko Grace Sally

Lisa Kay Emma Sophi Elena Nancy

Elisa Carol Yuko Pam Jessie Amber

B Speak. Choose someone in the classroom. Your partner will ask *yes/no* questions to find out who it is. Take turns.

Example:

A: Is she wearing a T-shirt?

B: Yes.

A: It's our teacher.

Working on Fluency ▶ Giving Advice Politely

Compliment	Advice
I like your jeans,	**but I think you should** wear a skirt.
Your black pants are nice,	**but why don't you try something** brighter?

A 🔘 **20 Listen.** Yumi and Luis are talking about their styles. Draw or write what clothes they should wear.

Yumi's New Style

Luis's New Style

B Write. Think of two things you want to change about your own style. Use these ideas or others of your own.

▸ more like a college student ▸ shorter/taller ▸ younger/older ▸ more feminine

▸ more serious/less serious ▸ more fashionable ▸ bigger/thinner

1. I want to look _____.

2. I _____.

C Speak. Ask some classmates what they want to change and give some advice.

Example:
A: What do you want to change?
B: I want to look more fashionable.
A: Well, your sandals are nice, but I think you should try dress shoes.

Challenge

Interview your partner and design a new look. Then, tell the class about your partner's current and new styles.

A Write. Look at what your partner is wearing today. Make some notes. Then, before you interview your partner, think of some questions to ask.

What my partner is wearing:

_____

_____

_____

My interview questions:

1. How do you want to change your look?

_____

_____

_____

_____

B Speak. Interview your partner. Ask your questions and other follow-up questions. Take notes on what your partner says.

Example:

A: So, how do you want to change your look?

B: I want to look more feminine and sophisticated.

A: Do you like to wear dresses to school?

Critical Thinking

Think about how to ask your questions politely before you interview your partner. When should you use "May I ask?" How can you introduce advice in a polite way?

C Prepare. Write your style makeover script. Then draw your partner's "current look" and "new look."

Introduce yourself:	Hi, I'm _____'s stylist.
Describe your partner's current look:	Today, _____ is wearing . . .
Explain what you learned about your partner:	In the interview, he/she said . . .
Describe your partner's new look:	Now, he/she is wearing . . .

Ana's Current Look

The Movie Star Look

D Present. Tell other students about your partners' current and new styles.

Presentation Tip

Make eye contact with your audience — your audience will feel like you are really talking to them.

Reflection Time

Write useful words and ideas you learned in this unit.

When You Have Time ▸ Extra Activities

If you finish an activity in this unit before your classmates, try one of these.

A Unscramble the clothing words.

1. trski   _skirt_
2. sanpt   _____
3. dssaanl   _____
4. sneja   _____
5. eeatsrw   _____
6. eatkjc   _____

B Do the fashion fads quiz.

_____ 1960s, ironing hair
_____ 1950s, bouffant hairstyles
_____ 1990s, platform shoes
_____ 1980s, leisure suits
_____ 1940s, zoot suits
_____ 1970s, afro haircuts

C Talk with a partner about your style.

1. Do you have a favorite clothes designer or brand? If so, which one?
2. What styles of clothes do you dislike?
3. What are your favorite colors for clothes?
4. What colors do not suit you?

Level Up

When you describe a clothing item, you can give an opinion and mention the size as well. Usually, the adjectives follow this order: **1.** opinion, **2.** size, **3.** color, **4.** design/material. For example,

▸ a beautiful, short cotton skirt

Put each of these adjectives in the right category. Then write descriptions for the items below.

> short   large   lovely   traditional
> fashionable   long   beautiful   small

Opinion	**Size**
_____	_____
_____	_____
_____	_____
_____	_____

1. sweatshirt / large / gray / cotton
   _a_____
2. denim / blue / short / jacket
   _____
3. striped / fashionable / blue and white / T-shirt
   _____
4. long / black / beautiful / dress
   _____
5. Your idea:
   _____

Honesty

Hi Mom! What am I doing? I'm studying with some friends.

☐ to your parents about what you are doing

Thanks. I love it!

☐ to someone who gives you a bad gift

Unit Challenge

▸ Tell short stories about difficult situations.
▸ Discuss what you would do.

Warm Up

A Check [✓]. Which lies do you think are OK to tell?

B Speak. Compare your answers with a partner. Give more information.

Example:

A: Do you think it's OK to tell a lie to your parents about what you are doing?

B: Maybe. I'm not sure. How about you?

A: No way! I think it's wrong.

Where's your homework?

My computer crashed.

☐ to a teacher

Yes. It's really . . . interesting.

Do you like my new hairstyle?

☐ to a friend about his or her style

Challenge Preview

A 🔘 **21** **Listen.** Kirsten and her group are discussing a difficult situation. Who would tell the truth?

☐ Ethan

☐ Luis

☐ Sang-mi

Here's my story. What would you do in this situation?

Hmmm . . .

B 🔘 **21** **Write and listen again.** Fill in the missing verbs. Then listen and check your ideas.

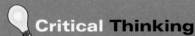

asks   think   likes   gets   tell

Kirsten: Here's my story. What would you do in this situation? Your best friend _____ a new **hairstyle**. She _____ it a lot, but you _____ it's really **bad**. Then, she _____ you "Do you like my new **hairstyle**?" Would you _____ her the truth? How about you, Luis?

Luis: No way! I'd say "It's **interesting**."

C **Speak.** Practice the conversation with a partner. Then change the words in **red** and talk about this photo.

💡 Critical Thinking

Luis doesn't want to hurt his friend's feelings. What else can he say?

▶ hat
▶ ugly
▶ "It's unique."

Working on Language ▶ Asking Hypothetical Questions

> **Would you (ever)** skip school to do something fun?
>
> Sure, why not?
> No, I wouldn't.
> Maybe. It depends.

A Write. How honest are you? Answer these questions ✓ = Yes, ✗ = No, or ? = Maybe.

1. ☐ skip class to do something fun?

2. ☐ take someone else's umbrella?

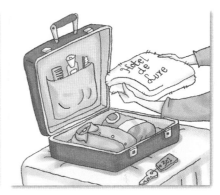

3. ☐ take a "souvenir" from a hotel or restaurant?

4. ☐ send text messages during class?

5. ☐ tell a teacher you're sick when you're not?

6. ☐ keep money you find on the street?

B Write Think of two more questions using "Would you ever."

1. _____

2. _____

C Speak. Ask a partner the questions in activities A and B.

Example:

A: Would you skip class to do something fun?

B: Maybe. It depends. What class?

A: Math class.

B: Sure.

Communicate ▶ What Would You Do?

A Write. What would you do in these situations? Fill in the answers to questions 2 and 3.

Example: You see a classmate cheating on a test.

> tell the teacher / not do anything

What would you do?

I would tell the teacher.

Why? / Why not?

It's wrong to cheat.

Level Up!
See page 106.

1. You find a diamond ring in the park.

> keep it / give it to the police

What would you do?

_____

Why? / Why not?

_____

Useful Expressions

I could never do that.
It's wrong.
Lots of people do it.
It's not my problem.
It's his/her own fault.

2. You break something in a store.

> pay for it / not say anything

What would you do?

_____

Why? / Why not?

_____

B Speak. Ask a partner the questions above. Ask "Why?" or "Why not?".

Example:

A: You see some classmates cheating on a test. What would you do?

B: I wouldn't do anything.

A: Why?

B: It's not my problem.

A classmate asks
to copy your homework.

You hear gossip
about your friend.

A store clerk gives
you too much change.

Working on Fluency ▶ Asking for Clarification

A 🔘 **22** **Listen.** Marco is asking Grace for some advice. Which picture shows Marco's problem? Check [✓] the correct picture.

1. ☐
2. ☐
3. ☐

B 🔘 **22** **Listen again.** Grace asks some questions to get more information. Check [✔] the three questions you hear.

1. ☐ Did you say advice?
2. ☐ What do you mean by "ex"?
3. ☐ Like where, for example?
4. ☐ Do you mean your last girlfriend?
5. ☐ What kind of restaurant?
6. ☐ How jealous?

> 💡 **Critical Thinking**
>
> Think about the situation in activity A. What advice would you give Marco? Why? What would you tell him?

C **Speak.** Choose one of these complaints or think of one of your own. Tell a partner and give more information.

I hate it when . . .
▶ people use my things without asking.
▶ people get angry.
▶ people don't keep secrets.

Example:
A: I hate it when people use my things without asking.
B: Like what, for example?
A: Well, my bicycle and my computer.

Challenge

Describe a difficult situation and then ask your classmates what they would do.

A Check [✓]. Read the story and decide what you would do.

Your boss asks you to work on Sunday so that he can go to his daughter's wedding. But Sunday is your birthday and your friends are planning a party for you. What would you do in this situation?

☐ I would say I'm sick and go to the party.

☐ I would work and say I'm sorry to my friends.

☐ I would tell my boss the truth and ask to go.

☐ I would _____.

B Write. Prepare your own story.

YOUR STORY:

C Speak. Tell your story to your classmates. Ask what they would do and why. Write their answers down.

Name	What he/she would do	Why?

Reflection Time

Write useful words and ideas you learned in this unit.

When You Have Time ▶ Extra Activities

If you finish an activity in this unit before your classmates, try one of these.

A Find the words in **bold** in the word search.

1. tell a **lie**
2. a difficult **situation**
3. **cheat** on a test
4. **skip** school
5. a **jealous** boyfriend
6. **steal** something
7. It **depends**.
8. In that **case** . . .

N	L	J	C	D	Y	K	T	D	B	T	O	X	X	Z	Q
H	R	A	T	H	I	B	B	C	S	P	X	B	N	T	M
O	P	B	I	O	E	H	W	R	X	K	J	G	X	U	H
D	N	S	O	L	C	A	F	E	E	Q	I	B	H	D	I
E	C	F	Y	J	Z	A	T	C	L	A	S	P	A	T	G
P	D	A	C	Z	S	T	E	A	L	R	S	E	F	D	C
E	P	X	S	C	P	L	A	E	J	E	A	L	O	U	S
N	Y	G	V	E	D	A	I	X	O	H	F	S	P	W	P
D	N	K	J	X	K	L	J	E	U	A	L	R	O	S	L
S	P	S	I	T	U	A	T	I	O	N	W	K	Z	L	P

B How big are these problems? Rank these problems from the most serious (1) to the least serious (6).

Your girlfriend/ boyfriend:

_____ promises to call you, but doesn't.

_____ is an hour late for a date.

_____ forgets your birthday.

_____ is mad at you but won't tell you why.

_____ has lunch with an "ex."

_____ spends more time with friends than with you.

C Talk with a partner about problems and difficult situations.

1. What's a difficult situation you have had recently? How did you solve it?
2. Who do you talk to when you have a problem?
3. Are you good at giving advice to your friends?
4. What would you do if a friend called you in the middle of the night to talk about a problem?

Level Up

Make these sentences into questions.
Example: You see someone cheating on a test.

▶ **What would you do if** you <u>saw</u> someone cheating on a test?

Notice how the verb changes. Change these sentences into questions and ask your partner.

1. You find a diamond ring in the park.

_____

_____

2. You break something in a store.

_____

_____

3. A classmate asks to copy your homework.

_____

_____

4. A store clerk gives you too much change.

_____

_____

5. You hear some gossip about a friend.

_____

_____

Making Things Better

The location is great.

The classes are interesting.

The campus is beautiful.

The students are fun.

The teachers are friendly.

Unit Challenge

▸ Discuss problems at school.
▸ Do a group presentation.

Warm Up

A Check [✓]. What do you like about your school?

B Speak. Ask your classmates what they like about school. Do you agree?

Example:
A: What do you like about our school?
B: Well, the location is great. It's very convenient for me.
A: Really? It takes me an hour to get here.

Challenge Preview

A 🔘 **23 Listen.** Yumi and her group are explaining a problem at school, and suggesting their solution. What is their solution?

☐ build a new cafeteria
☐ open an Indian restaurant
☐ set up some food stalls

Today, we're going to present our idea to improve school life.

B 🔘 **23 Listen again.** Write "more," "too many," or "enough" in the blanks.

Yumi: First, **Ana** is going to tell you about the problem at our school, **City University**. **Ana**?

Ana: Here's the problem: we don't have _____ places to eat lunch at **City U**, so the cafeteria is always crowded. There are _____ people and there isn't _____ time to eat lunch.

Yumi: Thanks, **Ana**. Next, **Kirsten** is going to explain our idea. **Kirsten**?

Kirsten: We need _____ places to eat, so we want to set up food stalls. One stall sells lunch boxes. Another stall sells sandwiches. And another one sells Indian food.

C Speak. Practice the conversation in groups of three. Then change the words in **red** and use your own names.

Working on Language ▶ Describing Problems

Problem	Effect
We don't have enough homework, **so**	I'm not learning much.
We have too much	I have to study every night.
There are not enough social events, **so**	I can't make new friends.
There are too many	I don't have time to study.

A Write. Think of some difficulties students have at your school. Use your own ideas or those below.

too much time between classes — get bored

too many students — can't talk to the teacher

a lot of exams — always stressed out

Example: <u>There is too much time between classes, so I get bored.</u>

1. _____

2. _____

3. _____

4. _____

B Speak. Talk with a partner about the biggest problems for you.

Example:

A: I think there's too much time between classes, so I get bored.

B: Really? That doesn't bother me.

> **Useful Expressions**
>
> I think so too.
> I agree. I don't like that either.
> Really? I doesn't bother me.

Communicate ▶ That's a Great Idea!

A Write. Read the problem and the students' suggestions. What are some other solutions you can think of? Compare your ideas with a partner.

I get sleepy in class. What should I do to stay awake?

You could stand up or stretch when you get sleepy.

Or you could drink some coffee before class.

1. _____

2. _____

B Speak. Get in groups and read these problems. Try to give solutions. Write down all your ideas on a piece of paper. The group with the most ideas for each problem is the winner.

Useful **Expressions**

That's a good idea.
Nice!
What else should I do?

Example:

A: I don't have many friends at school. What should I do?

B: You could join a club.

I don't have classes between 10 a.m. and 2 p.m. What should I do?

I have trouble waking up in the morning. What should I do?

I don't have many friends at school. What should I do?

I can't remember new English words. What should I do?

Working on Fluency ▶ Encouraging Others to Speak

A 🔘 **24** **Listen.** A college baseball team is discussing how to use some money. Check [✓] the two ideas they discuss.

1. ☐   2. ☐   3. ☐   4. ☐

B 🔘 **24** **Listen again.** Check [✓] the questions and expressions you hear.

Encouraging people to start talking:	Encouraging people to continue talking:
☐ Who wants to start?	☐ Good. Tell me more.
☐ Well Ana, how about you?	☐ Uh-huh.
☐ Does anyone else have an idea?	☐ Yeah.
☐ What do you think, Yumi?	☐ Right.

C **Speak.** Get into groups of four and discuss the school bulletin. Change the discussion leader for each suggestion. Use the language above to encourage others to speak.

Level Up! See page 114.

Good news!
A billionaire gave your school a million dollars. You can use it to:

1. Make a new building
2. Buy sports equipment
3. Have parties and events
4. Improve the classrooms

💡 **Critical Thinking**

Think about what makes a good discussion leader. What are the three most important things a discussion leader should do? Make a list.

Example:

A: What kind of new building can we make? Who would like to start?

B: We could open an ice cream shop.

A: Uh-huh. What do you think, Frankie?

C: Yes, we could make our own ice cream.

Challenge

In groups, think of an idea to improve your school and present to the class.

A Write and speak. Think of some problems at your school that you would like to discuss with your classmates. Then get into groups, and choose one idea to work on.

Example: There aren't enough chances to speak English.

1. _____
2. _____

B Speak. Choose a discussion leader for your group. Then discuss solutions and write them down.

Example: not enough chances to speak English

Ideas:

1. Start an English table
2. Start a class blog or an English book club

Your notes:

C Prepare.
In groups, choose the best solution and prepare a group presentation. Give each student a different role, like the ones below. Then practice.

Examples of roles:
- ▶ explain the problem
- ▶ explain one solution
- ▶ explain another solution
- ▶ explain a picture
- ▶ give a summary
- ▶ ask audience for ideas

Names and Roles	The Problem

The Solution

D Present.
Give your presentation to the class. The audience will ask questions. Then, vote on the best ideas for the class.

Presentation Tip

Use visual aids (pictures, maps, drawings, etc.) to help the audience understand your presentation.

They also help you remember what to say. But don't just hold them, point to the key parts as you speak.

Reflection Time

Write useful words and ideas you learned in this unit.

When You Have Time ▶ Extra Activities

If you finish an activity in this unit before your classmates, try one of these.

A Where are these universities? Write the country.

The United States	New Zealand
Peru	Egypt
Scotland	England
Spain	France

1. The Sorbonne

_____

2. The University of Cambridge

_____

3. The University of Otago

_____

4. Stanford University

_____

5. National University of San Marcos

_____

6. Al-Azhar University

_____

7. University of Salamanca

_____

8. University of St. Andrews

_____

B Take the school dropout quiz. Which of these famous people dropped out of (quit) school?

☐ Keanu Reeves (actor)
☐ George Harrison (Beatles singer)
☐ Jim Carrey (comedian, actor)
☐ Cher (singer, actor)
☐ Sean Connery (actor)
☐ Tom Cruise (actor)

C Talk with a partner about study habits.

1. What's your favorite school subject?
2. What subjects do you dislike?
3. Do you always do your homework?
4. How many hours per week do you study?

Level Up

You can use these phrases to offer a different opinion.

▸ Yes, I like that idea, but on the other hand . . .
▸ Well, I agree with you, but . . .
▸ That's interesting, but I think a better idea is to . . .
▸ I know what you mean, but . . .

Work with a partner. One person gives an opinion about school. The other person offers a different opinion using the phrases above.

Example:

A: I think students should decide the topic of every lesson.

B: Yes, I like that idea, but on the other hand, it makes life difficult for the teacher.

What I Learned

Make a poster about what you learned in this course and tell others about it.

A Discuss. These students are talking about their experiences studying English. Are you the same as these people? How have you changed?

At the beginning of this course I was really shy. Now I'm more confident about talking to people in English.

I used to think English was hard and I didn't like studying. Now I enjoy English more. I made some good friends in this class.

I didn't like to speak English because I made mistakes. Now I don't worry about that so much. I learned a lot in this class, but I was absent sometimes.

B Prepare. Complete the chart and then write notes about your experiences studying English.

1. Check [✓] the statements that are true for you.

1. I worked hard in this class.	
2. I learned a lot of new English words.	
3. I can speak English more fluently now.	
4. I made some new friends in this class.	
5. I enjoy studying English more than I used to.	
6. I usually had fun in this class.	

2. Write words or sentences about these things.

What you were like before this class

_____

The best thing about this class

_____

Something you did a good job on

_____

Something you got better at

_____

What you are like now

_____

The hardest thing about this class

_____

Something important you learned

_____

Something you want to do better at

_____

C **Create.** Look at your answers in B and make a poster. Choose the most important points you want to put on your poster.

What I Learned
by Wayne Goody

A lot of friends

✓ Favorite class: Radio DJ project
✓ More confident
✓ Able to speak better English
✓ Worked hard on my presentations

D **Present.** Show your poster to your classmates and tell them about it.

AUDIO SCRIPTS

🔘 1 Unit 1 Challenge Preview

Kirsten: Hi, I'm Kirsten. **What's your** name?

Luis: I'm Luis. Nice to meet you, Kirsten.

Kirsten: It's nice to meet you, too. So Luis, may I ask you some questions?

Luis: Sure, Kirsten.

Kirsten: Um, **what's your** last name, Luis?

Luis: It's Garcia.

Kirsten: How do you spell that?

Luis: G-A-R-C-I-A.

Kirsten: Did you say G-A-R-C-I-A?

Luis: Yes, that's right.

Kirsten: OK. **What's your** cell phone number?

Luis: It's 090-555-1212.

Kirsten: Can you say that again, please?

Luis: Sure. 090-555-1212.

Kirsten: OK, I got it.

🔘 2 Unit 1 Working on Fluency

1. Man: Hey, Julie.

Woman: Hi, Ryan. What's up?

Man: May I ask what your cell phone number is?

Woman: Oh, sure. It's 090-555-6417.

Man: Thanks, Julie.

Woman: *I don't usually tell people my phone number, but we're classmates, so why not? Maybe we can help each other sometimes.*

2. Woman: Hi, Andrew. May I ask you a personal question?

Man: Sure, please do.

Woman: You're really big. How tall are you?

Man: I'm 192 centimeters. *People always want to know my height. Her question didn't bother me at all. After all, I am big.*

3. Man: Hi, Emma. Nice to meet you.

Woman: Hi.

Man: Hey, I'd really like to know . . . how old are you?

Woman: Hmm. Sorry. I'd rather not say. *I hate talking about my age because I'm 26. I'm a few years older than the other students.*

Spoken English: Table of Contents

When speaking, native speakers of American English often change the way they pronounce certain phrases. In this section, there are examples of:

1. What's your ▶ "Watsyer"
2. Do you ▶ "Doya"
3. want to ▶ "wanna"; going to ▶ "gonna"
4. Let me ▶ "Lemme"
5. used to ▶ "useta"
6. Can you ▶ "Canya"
7. What's up? ▶ "Wassup?"
8. What are you ▶ "Waddaya"
9. kinds of ▶ "kindsa"; kind of ▶ "kinda"
10. I don't know ▶ "I dunno"
11. Would you ▶ "Wudja"
12. What do you ▶ "Waddaya"

Spoken English: What's your ▶ "Watsyer"

A. Listen to these questions on the audio
CD: **What's your** name?
What's your last name, Luis?
What's your cell phone number?

B. Now practice these questions:
1. What's your address?
2. What's your email address?
3. What's your middle name?
4. What's your favorite food?

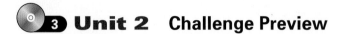

3 Unit 2 Challenge Preview

Yumi: Hi, Ethan.

Ethan: Hi, Yumi. This is a picture of me when I was in high school.

Yumi: OK. Who's this?

Ethan: That's my friend, Andrew.

Yumi: Where were you?

Ethan: Um, we were at a baseball game.

Yumi: Was it fun?

Ethan: Yeah, it was a great day.

Yumi: **Do you** still see Andrew?

Ethan: Sometimes. He's a cool guy.

4 Unit 2 Working on Fluency

Kirsten: Well, this is a picture of my sister, Mary. It's one of my favorite photos.

Steven: She's cute. May I ask you some questions?

Kirsten: Sure, please do.

Steven: How old is she?

Kirsten: She's 13.

Steven: Where did you take it?

Kirsten: Um, at the park near our house.

Steven: Is that a volleyball?

Kirsten: Yes, it is.

Steven: Did she have a game that day?

Kirsten: Yeah, a BIG game. I took this before the game started.

Steven: So she likes volleyball. Is that her favorite sport?

Kirsten: It was. Now she's into soccer.

Steven: Oh, soccer . . . **Do you** have any other sisters?

Kirsten: No, just Mary. One sister is enough!

Spoken English: Do you ▸ "Doya"

A. Listen to these questions on the audio CD: **Do you** still see Andrew?

Do you have any other sisters?

B. Now practice these questions:

1. Do you want to see my photos?
2. Do you have any pets?
3. Do you like studying English?
4. Do you live alone?

5 Unit 3 Challenge Preview

Steven: So, Sang-mi, what's something you'd like to do in the future?

Sang-mi: I'd like to go to Thailand this winter.

Steven: Really? Why?

Sang-mi: Because I **want to** learn how to cook Thai food.

Steven: So, what's your plan?

Sang-mi: Well, tonight, I'm **going to** find a cooking school on the Internet.

Steven: That's a good idea.

Sang-mi: Then, by November, I'm **going to** book my ticket and a hotel room.

Steven: That sounds good too, Sang-mi.

6 Unit 3 Working on Fluency

Yumi: What's something you'd like to do, Luis?

Luis: I really **want to** go to Australia next summer and study English.

Yumi: That sounds good.

Luis: So what should I do? Do you have any suggestions?

Ana: Well, I think you should go to a language school in Sydney.

Luis: Really? Why?

Ana: Oh, it's a fantastic city. I did a home stay there two years ago and had a great time.

Yumi: I think you should take the TOEFL test. Some schools ask for a TOEFL score when you apply.

Luis: OK. That's a good idea.

Ethan: I think you should talk to a travel agency.

Luis: About air tickets?

Ethan: Yeah, and ask about discount tickets. You should try to get a cheap ticket.

Luis: Good idea. Thanks.

Spoken English: want to ▶ "wanna"; going to ▶ "gonna"

A. Listen to these items on the audio CD:
  I **want to** learn how to cook Thai food.
  I'm **going to** find a cooking school.
  I'm **going to** book my ticket.
  I really **want to** go to Australia.

B. Now practice these sentences:
  1. I want to be famous someday.
  2. They want to be fluent in English.
  3. He's going to move to a different city.
  4. She's going to live abroad in the future.

Unit 4 **Challenge Preview**

Ethan: Steven, have you ever eaten anything strange?

Steven: Yes, I have. **Let me** tell you about it.
Last summer, I took a trip to Canada. One day, I went into a forest. I found an apple and ate it. But there was a bug inside the apple, so I ate that too!

Kirsten: Really?

Steven: Uh-huh. It was awful.

Ethan: Really?

Sang-mi: I believe you.

Kirsten: Me too.

Ethan: Oh, I don't. It's a lie.

Steven: It's not true. You were right, Ethan.

Unit 4 **Working on Fluency**

Yumi: **Let me** tell you about an amazing man I met.

Luis: OK.

Yumi: One day, I went to the river near my home. I walked along the river and came to a bridge.

Luis: Uh-huh.

Yumi: There was a homeless man under the bridge. I was shocked. The poor man had a house made from a cardboard box. And guess what? He had about 20 dogs.

Luis: Oh, that sounds scary.

Yumi: So I asked, "Why do you have so many dogs?" and he said "These dogs are homeless too. I take care of them." Every day, he looked for food for the dogs.

Luis: Really?

Yumi: And some of the dogs were very sick. He even asked strangers for money to buy medicine.

Luis: Oh, that's sad.

Yumi: It was so touching. The man was poor and homeless, but he tried so hard to help those dogs.

Luis: Thanks, Yumi. That's a great story.

Spoken English: Let me ▶ "Lemme"

A. Listen to these items on the audio CD:
   Let me tell you about it.
   Let me tell you about an amazing man I met.

B. Now practice these sentences:
   1. Let me tell you about my trip to Thailand.
   2. Let me tell you about a movie I saw.
   3. Let me tell you about a concert I went to.
   4. Let me tell you about my pet dog.

9 Unit 5 Challenge Preview

Ana: So, Ethan. Let me give you a tour of my hometown.

Ethan: OK.

Ana: Well, there was a river near my house. It was really beautiful.

Ethan: Why is that place special for you?

Ana: I **used to** go there with my boyfriend.

Ethan: How often did you go?

Ana: Hmm, every day, usually.

Ethan: That sounds nice. What did you do there?

Ana: We **used to** talk about our dreams and college—you know, the future.

Ethan: Do you still go there?

Ana: Yes, sometimes.

Ethan: Thanks for telling me about that.

10 Unit 5 Working on Fluency

Now, you're going to do a relaxation exercise. It will help you remember a place, or maybe a person or an event from your past. Are you ready? Close your eyes and listen. Take a deep breath and relax.

Think about somewhere you **used to** go. Where did you go? Think of that place. Can you see it? What are some of the things you can see? Relax. Take deep breaths. Remember the place. See it in your mind. Now smell. Breathe in deeply. What happened to you there? Remember it. See it in your mind. Take a deep breath. What can you smell?

Now listen. Listen and remember. What sounds can you hear? Is there someone talking? What are they saying? Can you hear any sounds in the distance?

Relax. Think about your feelings. How did you feel? Were you happy? Or, were you sad? Relax and remember how you felt.

OK. Slowly, I'm going to bring you back. Slowly . . . Slowly . . . open your eyes. OK. What did you remember?

Spoken English: used to ▶ "useta"

A. Listen to these items on the audio CD:

I **used to** go there with my boyfriend.

We **used to** talk about our dreams and college.

Think about somewhere you **used to** go.

B. Now practice these sentences:

1. We used to sit by the river and talk.
2. I used to go to the park when I was little.
3. She used to play baseball when I was in high school.
4. He used to go to the Lincoln movie theater.

Sang-mi:	Hello. May I help you?
Steven:	Yes, please. **Can you** tell me about this watch?
Sang-mi:	Oh, this watch is real gold. It's beautiful, isn't it?
Steven:	Yes, it is.
Sang-mi:	It's a very popular brand. And it's a reasonable price too.
Steven:	Really? How much is it?
Sang-mi:	It's $200.
Steven:	That's too much. **Can you** give me a better price?
Sang-mi:	OK. I can let you have it for $180.
Steven:	**Can you** make it $150?
Sang-mi:	OK. It's a deal.
Steven:	Thanks.

Man:	Hi, I'm Rick Jeeves. I'm in Vancouver at Canada's biggest flea market. Today, I'm going to buy a camera. Listen to how I bargain.
Woman:	May I help you?
Man:	*I went to other shops and compared prices before coming to this shop.* Umm, how much is this camera?
Woman:	This one? Oh, that's a very high quality camera. It's only $100.
Man:	*That's too much, so I'll ask for a lower price.* That's high. **Can you** give me a better price?
Woman:	Well, how about $90?
Man:	*Hmmm. That's not good. I'll offer a really low price.* Thanks, but that's too much. How about $50?
Woman:	$50? Oh, I'm sorry. That's too low. How about $75?
Man:	No, sorry. Well, thanks anyway. *I'm walking away.*
Woman:	No, no wait. Come back. OK. I can let you have this camera for $70.
Man:	What? Oh, $70. All right. I'll take it. So, from $100 to $70. Now that is a good price. I'm Rick Jeeves. Happy bargaining!

Spoken English: Can you ▶ "Canya"

A. Listen to these questions on the audio CD: **Can you** tell me about this watch?
Can you give me a better price?
Can you make it $150?

B. Now practice these questions:
1. Can you help me, please?
2. Can you give me a discount?
3. Can you tell me about this necklace?
4. Can you give me a lower price?

13 Unit 7 Challenge Preview

Yumi:	So, what's your gift, Ana?
Ana:	Oh, I have the perfect gift for my friend. I'd like to give Emma a one-year study trip to the United States.
Yumi:	Uh-huh.
Ana:	Her school gave her a scholarship when she was in high school, but she couldn't go.
Yumi:	Really?
Ana:	Yes, her father got sick, so she had to take care of him.
Yumi:	That's too bad.
Ana:	Emma really wanted to study abroad, and it's still her dream. So, I want to give her that chance.
Yumi:	That's a lovely gift, Ana.

14 Unit 7 Working on Fluency

Kirsten:	Thanks for inviting me to dinner, Ethan.
Ethan:	You're welcome, Kirsten. I really enjoyed it. Anyway, Kirsten . . .
Kirsten:	Yes?
Ethan:	I have a present for you.
Kirsten:	For me? You shouldn't have. Can I open it?
Ethan:	Yes, of course. Please do.
Kirsten:	Oh, it's a ring.
Ethan:	Do you like it?
Kirsten:	Yes. It's beautiful. I love it. Thank you so much.
Ethan:	You're welcome . . .
Kirsten:	Hello.
Ethan:	Hi, Kirsten. It's Ethan.
Kirsten:	Hey, Ethan. **What's up?**
Ethan:	So, are we going out tonight?
Kirsten:	Tonight? Um, I can't. I'm meeting Joey tonight.
Ethan:	Joey? I thought . . .
Kirsten:	What?
Ethan:	Well, you know, I gave you that ring and . . .
Kirsten:	Yeah, I'm wearing it now. I really like it.
Ethan:	I guess, well, I guess I'd like it back.
Kirsten:	Why? I thought it was a gift.
Ethan:	It was. But I thought you were my girlfriend.
Kirsten:	Girlfriend? Um, no. I . . .

Spoken English: What's up? ▶ "Wassup?"

A. Listen to this greeting on the audio CD: **What's up?**

B. Now practice these questions:
1. What's up, Kirsten?
2. What's up, Darren?

🔘15 Unit 8 Challenge Preview

Sang-mi: We're having a barbecue on Saturday. Can you come?

Luis: Hmm, Saturday? I'm a little busy this weekend. Who's going to come?

Sang-mi: I'm inviting everyone from our English class.

Luis: So, **what are you** going to do?

Sang-mi: Well, we're going to cook some burgers and hot dogs.

Luis: What else are you going to do?

Sang-mi: Yumi's band is going to play for us too.

Luis: Hey, that sounds fun. What time does it start?

Sang-mi: At about 7:30. So can you come?

Luis: Sure. I'd love to. Thanks for inviting me.

🔘16 Unit 8 Working on Fluency

1. Woman: Let's surprise her when she gets home. We can turn off the lights and hide.

Man: Yeah, I like it. She's going to be so surprised.

2. Man: Hmm. What should we do after Elisa and Hiroshi cut the cake?

Woman: Oh, I have an idea. Let's make them feed the cake to each other!

Man: That's a good idea. That'll be funny.

3. Man: So, **what are you** going to wear?

Woman: Let's dress up together in a horse costume. I'll be the head and you be the tail.

Man: OK. How about this instead? I'LL be the head and YOU be the tail.

4. Woman 1: Let's do this. We get some DVDs, make popcorn, and watch movies all night.

Woman 2: Well, I'm not sure. You always fall asleep.

Woman 1: No problem. I can stay awake if I want to.

Spoken English: What are you ▶ "Waddaya"

A. Listen to these questions on the audio CD: **What are you** going to do?
  What are you going to wear?

B. Now practice these questions:
  1. What are you going to eat at the party?
  2. What are you going to bring?
  3. What are you doing after the party?
  4. What are you planning to do?

Sang-mi: Hi, everybody. I interviewed Yumi about her musical tastes. Yumi said she loves all **kinds of** music and listens to it all the time. Yumi is really into hip-hop, and she's crazy about the group "Black Eyed Peas." "Where is the Love?" is one of her favorite songs, and it reminds her of her high school. Yumi saw "Black Eyed Peas" in concert last year. She said they were amazing. The most interesting thing Yumi told me is she wrote a hip-hop song in English! I think that's really cool!

Woman: So, may I ask you a few questions, Lamon?

Man: Sure. Go ahead.

Woman: What **kind of** music do you like?

Man: Well, I really like punk.

Woman: Do you like any other **kinds of** music?

Man: Um, not really. Rock is OK. But I hate pop and country.

Woman: So, how did you get into punk?

Man: My parents had so many punk albums. One day, I played one and . . . wow! I loved it.

Woman: Well, I don't know much about punk. Who do you recommend?

Man: You should listen to "The Ramones" first—you should start with them.

Woman: Why? Who are they?

Man: They were a New York punk band in the 1970s.

Woman: OK, so can you recommend one "Ramones" song? What do you think is their best song?

Man: I recommend "Blitzkrieg Bop." It's one of my favorites.

Woman: Oh really, why?

Man: I love the lyrics: "Hey! Ho! Let's Go!"

Woman: OK, thanks for recommending that to me . . .

Spoken English: kinds of ▸ "kindsa"; kind of ▸ "kinda"

A. Listen to these questions on the audio CD: Yumi said she loves all **kinds of** music.
What **kind of** music do you like?
Do you like any other **kinds of** music?

B. Now practice these questions:
1. What's the best kind of music?
2. We're into the same kind of music.
3. I listen to various kinds of music.
4. She doesn't like any kind of music at all.

19 Unit 10 Challenge Preview

Steven: Hi, everybody. I'm Steven, Ethan's stylist. Today, I'm going to tell you about Ethan's "style makeover."
This is Ethan's "current look." Ethan is wearing brown cotton pants and a blue denim shirt. He's also wearing some white leather sneakers. It's a very casual look.
Ethan said he wants to look more fashionable. His favorite colors are black, blue, and white. In his new look, Ethan is wearing black denim jeans, a white long-sleeved shirt, and a black leather vest. He's also wearing brown leather cowboy boots and a cowboy hat from the United States. It's a fun, fashionable look. Ethan loves it!

Ethan: That's right, Steven. I love it.

Steven: So, what do you think?

20 Unit 10 Working on Fluency

1. Yumi: I want to look younger, so what should I wear? Do you have any suggestions?

Ethan: So, you want to look younger. Let me see.
Well, your green skirt looks nice, but why don't you try something brighter? How about a pink miniskirt?

Yumi: Are you sure? . . . OK. And I want to look taller too.

Ethan: Taller . . . I think you should wear a blouse with vertical stripes, you know, stripes that go up and down.

Yumi: OK, vertical stripes. Thanks, Ethan.

Ethan: You're welcome.

2. Ana: What do you want to change, Luis?

Luis: Hmm. **I don't know.** Let me think . . . Well, I want to look thinner because I'm a little heavy. What should I wear?

Ana: OK, I like your jeans, but I think you should wear something dark, like a black shirt. Lighter colors make people look big.

Luis: Ah, yes. I knew that. Good point.

Ana: And, wearing dots makes people look smaller too.

Luis: Dots? OK. Thanks, Ana.

Ana: It's my pleasure.

Spoken English: I don't know ▶ "I dunno"

A. Listen to this item on the audio CD: **I don't know.** Let me think.

B. Now practice these questions:
   1. I dunno what the answer is.
   2. I dunno what to say.

21 Unit 11 Challenge Preview

Kirsten: Here's my story. What **would you** do in this situation? Your best friend gets a new hairstyle. She likes it a lot, but you think it's really bad. Then, she asks you "Do you like my new hairstyle?" **Would you** tell her the truth? How about you, Luis?

Luis: No way! I'd say, "It's . . . interesting."

Kirsten: Why not tell her the truth?

Luis: Well, I don't want to hurt her feelings.

Kirsten: OK. How about you, Ethan? **Would you** tell her the truth?

Ethan: Maybe. It depends. What do you mean by "really bad"?

Kirsten: I mean, REALLY bad! It looks awful.

Ethan: Then, I probably would tell her the truth. After all, she's a good friend, right?

Kirsten: Right. And how about you, Sang-mi?

Sang-mi: Sure. I'd tell her the truth.

Luis: Sang-mi! Why?

Sang-mi: She looks stupid, right? So she needs to know.

22 Unit 11 Working on Fluency

Grace: Hello.

Marco: Hi, Grace. It's Marco.

Grace: Hey, what's up, Marco?

Marco: Well, I've got a problem. I need your advice.

Grace: Sure.

Marco: Well, I was downtown today, and I met my "ex."

Grace: What do you mean by "ex"?

Marco: I mean my ex-girlfriend. That girl I dated last year.

Grace: OK. I got it.

Marco: Anyway, she said she wanted to talk to me, so we went to a restaurant together.

Grace: What kind of restaurant?

Marco: Just a café. Anyway, should I tell my current girlfriend? What **would you** do?

Grace: You mean tell her about meeting your "ex"? I would. I hate it when people lie to me.

Marco: Well, she's really jealous.

Grace: How jealous?

Marco: She would probably break up with me.

Grace: That's really jealous.

Spoken English: Would you ▶ "Wudja"

A. Listen to these questions on the audio CD: What **would you** do in this situation? **Would you** tell her the truth? What **would you** do?

B. Now practice these questions:
1. Would you skip school to do something fun?
2. Would you take someone else's umbrella?
3. Would you send text messages during class?
4. Would you tell the teacher?

Unit 12 Challenge Preview

Yumi:	Hey, everybody! Today, we're going to present our idea to improve school life.
Steven:	Great, let's hear it.
Yumi:	First, Ana is going to tell you about the problem at our school, City University. Ana?
Ana:	Here's the problem: We don't have enough places to eat lunch at City U, so the cafeteria is always crowded—there are too many people and there isn't enough time to eat lunch.
Yumi:	Thanks, Ana. Next, Kirsten is going to explain our idea. Kirsten?
Kirsten:	We need more places to eat, so we want to set up food stalls. One stall sells lunch boxes. Another stall sells sandwiches. And another one sells Indian food.
Yumi:	Now, Ethan is going to show why this is a good idea. Ethan?
Ethan:	OK, look at this drawing. There are lines at each food stall, but the lines are short. And the cafeteria line is short too.
Yumi:	OK, well, thanks for listening. **What do you** think?

Unit 12 Working on Fluency

Steven:	OK, everyone. I've got some good news. The school soccer team has $1,000 to spend this year. How should we spend it? Who wants to start?
Luis:	Well, I've got an idea. We could have a big party, you know, with the cheerleaders.
Steven:	Sounds good. Does anyone else have an idea?
Kirsten:	Can I say something?
Steven:	Of course, Kirsten.
Kirsten:	We could buy new uniforms. Our uniforms are so old.
Steven:	Right.
Kirsten:	And we could get white uniforms next time, instead of blue ones.
Steven:	Nice idea! **What do you** think, Yumi?
Yumi:	Hmm. I think it's a great idea. Let's get new uniforms.
Kirsten:	I'm glad you like my idea. Do you like it too, Luis?
Luis:	I guess so, but I still want to have a party sometime.

Spoken English: What do you ▶ "Waddaya"

A. Listen to these questions on the audio
  CD: **What do you think?**
       What do you think, Yumi?

B. Now practice these questions:
  1. What do you want to discuss?
  2. What do you want to improve at school?
  3. What do you think we should do?
  4. What do you think about school?